W9-BRX-972

Table for One

The Savvy Girl's Guide to Singleness

Camerin Courtney

Fleming H. Revell
A Division of Baker Book House Co
Grand Rapids, Michigan 49516

Published by Fleming H. Revell
a division of Baker Publishing Group
P.O. Box 6287, Grand Rapids, MI 49516-6287

Fourth printing, March 2006

Printed in the United States of America

Library of Congress Cataloging-in-Publication Data
Courtney, Camerin, 1971–
    Table for one : the savvy girl's guide to singleness / Camerin
Courtney.
       p.   cm.
    ISBN 10: 0-8007-5795-5 (pbk.)
    ISBN 978-0-8007-5795-3 (pbk.)
    1. Single women—Psychology. 2. Interpersonal relations. 3. Single
women—Religious life. I. Title.
    HQ800.2 .C68   2002
    305.48´9652—dc21   2001007951

Table
for
One

Contents

Introduction   7

1. So, Why Aren't You Married Yet?   15
2. Antidotes for the Single Girl Blues   23
3. Singleness and Scripture   31
4. Solo on Sunday Morning   37
5. Singles Groupies and Dropouts   45
6. Home for the Holidays   53
7. Oh, Mother!   61
8. Leading Men   69
9. What Are Friends For?   77
10. We Are Family   85
11. Maternal Urges and Lusty Longings   95
12. This Isn't What I'd Expected   103
13. Three Reasons Why Men Aren't the Enemy   111
14. Male Bashing—And Other Guilty Pleasures   119
15. Bad Boys—Whatcha Gonna Do When They Come for You?   129
16. Going Solo   139
17. Where Do We Go from Here?   147

Introduction

*L*ife usually doesn't turn out the way we think it will. Take this book, for example. I was originally supposed to write it with a coworker of mine, Ginger. Actually, it was her idea. Working in Christian publishing, we'd seen our fair share of Christian singles books over the years— and to be honest, we'd been less than satisfied with the selection. The bulk seemed to be solely about finding the love of your life (as if that's the sum total of the single life) or were written by middle-aged, married male psychologists. Nothing against this genre as a whole, but what do they know about being a young(ish!) single woman in today's world? Ginger and I would occasionally joke that we should write the kind of gutsy, girly book we'd want to read if it appeared in our in-boxes.

Then one day, Ginger proposed that we do just that. It didn't take much for our brainstorming juices to flow, and several meetings at several different coffee shops later, we eventually had an outline. Then a full-blown proposal. And we finally got a Christian publishing company interested when, wouldn't you know it, Ginger's on-again, off-again boyfriend of six years finally saw the light and asked her to be his bride. Yea for her. Nay from the publisher. Having one of the authors be married kind of went against one of the main reasons we wanted to add another book to the slim singles section at the local Christian bookstore.

One of Ginger's last acts as a single woman was telling me to carry on without her. Not marrying until age thirty-two, she still believes strongly in spreading the message of happy, full-bodied singlehood. So I retooled the book as a solo act. A different publisher bit. And now you're holding the end result.

In the end, Ginger became a wife, and I became an author. What's cool is that both of us couldn't be happier. It's not like she won first place and I got the booby prize, though there was a time in my life when I would have seen it that way.

That was also a time when, if I found myself alone in a Blockbuster on a Friday or Saturday night, I'd feel compelled to look like I was picking out a flick for me and my "hot date" who I was meeting later in the evening. I'm not sure I ever achieved that "pre-date look" by being fully primped and checking my watch frequently (I was supposed to be meeting him later, get it?), but somehow between then and now I've become very comfortable having Me Nights. Now I bound into Blockbuster in sweats and a ball cap and select a flaming chick flick or subtitled artsy film with nary a care in the world that others may suspect I'll watch my selection while snarfing a Lean Cuisine dinner, sprawled on my living room floor—alone. (And love every minute of it!)

Why the change from self-conscious single girl to I-am-single-hear-me-roar woman? Over the past several years I've learned some valuable lessons about going solo in this paired-off world, not the least of which is that a happy, successful, God-pleasing life comes in many different packages. And contrary to what our churches, married friends, society, and nosy Aunt Marge may tell us, that includes singleness.

Ginger marrying the love of her life is a major "WooHoo" moment. But then so is fulfilling my lifelong dream of becoming an author. That's the whole point Ginger and I wanted to make in the first place—that there's a whole lot more to life than one's marital status. This is a lesson I've learned the hard way.

The One Who Got Away

Six years ago, I suffered the worst heartbreak of my life. I'd been dating "Andrew" off and on for three years, and I knew we needed to move forward in our relationship or move on. Despite the fact I'd met him at church on Valentine's Day, that he made me laugh and feel beautiful, that he loved God and his family, I still felt uncertain about moving toward marriage with this terrific guy.

I asked married friends what they felt before they got hitched. They all responded with some rendition of "I just knew he was the one," a feeling conspicuously absent in all my thinking and overanalyzing. I even met with a Christian counselor, who confirmed I wasn't a commitmentphobe. I prayed—no, pleaded—with God for direction. And when I was met with silence and a lack of peace for months on end, I slowly, excruciatingly, let the relationship go.

Without a tangible reason for the breakup, it's been easy for me to question the wisdom of my decision over the past six years. There were no "irreconcilable differences" or "I want kids and he doesn't"-type issues to blame, only a vague sense that God said no. I've alternated between seasons of peace (which, thankfully, have grown much longer over the years) and seasons of waning trust in God's grand plan. I haven't been obsessing, just wondering what to do with that nagging question mark in the back of my mind: *Was that really your leading, God?*

Well, God had his way of helping me deal with that question. I was on a shopping excursion a couple of summers ago when I saw Andrew across a trendy furniture store. There was a woman with him. Even though I hadn't seen Andrew in more than two years, I failed to muster the courage to walk over and say hello.

Later, kicking myself for being such a chicken, I chatted with God about this "chance" encounter. *Were you wanting us to get back together, God? Was it just bad timing before?* The what-ifs crept in big time, and I prayed once again for peace and direction. I could count on one hand the number of guys I'd dated in the six years since the breakup. When I let Andrew go, I'd assumed there would be someone even better waiting around the next corner. When that didn't prove true, I began to doubt my decision—and God's apparent leading.

I remember telling God it would almost be a relief to know the woman in the furniture store with Andrew was his wife. That would put the maddening questions to rest once and for all.

Well, about six months later I had another "chance" encounter, this time with a woman from my Bible study. We were chatting about work when she casually mentioned she knew Andrew. She'd even dated him briefly. She still saw him on occasion at work and knew he'd just gotten married a few weeks before.

I stood there in stunned silence, an odd mixture of grief and peace washing over me, feeling the clarity of a closed door and the loneliness of an empty horizon all at once. Yet I was amazed at the way God had orchestrated this answer to my prayer. While it wasn't a confirmation that the past decision to let Andrew go was absolutely God's will, it gave me peace with which to look to the future. And, I've learned, sometimes that's all we can hope for.

Learning of Andrew's marriage was a difficult yet unmistakable reminder that God's got it all in control—breakups and weddings, what-ifs and answers to prayer, and someday, if it's in his plan, the arrival of my Mr. Right. God once again proved he's there, listening, caring about my future. And this truth will be welcome company whether my expectations for the future are met—or not.

Would You Like Help with All That Baggage?

One of the best things I did after the demise of my relationship with Andrew was remain in counseling. Somehow God opened my tear-drenched eyes enough to see that all of us fallen human beings come with issues. Since I suddenly had a lot more free time on my hands, it seemed as good a time as any to tackle these issues, with the help of my wonderful Christian counselor, Linda. Together Linda, who didn't marry until age twenty-nine, and I looked at my childhood, my family, my people-pleasing tendencies, my expectations for life, God's role in all this, and so much more. In one-hour increments over the months and years that followed, I began to see myself and my erroneous thoughts about marriage and singleness more clearly. I began to make peace with my disappointments, my expectations, and my God. Slowly I began to stand on my own two feet, leaning on God's grand plan for my life, trusting his will over my own thoughts and schemes. Finally the day came when I realized I'd emerged single, strong, and unashamed (at least more days than not!).

Once I'd made peace with my singleness, I was free to embrace it and all the opportunities that came along with it. One of the best of these opportunities was becoming the singles columnist for ChristianityToday.com's Singles Channel. While part of me wanted to bolt from the dubious honor of being a spokesperson for singleness, the rest of me was intrigued at the prospect of becoming "SingleWoman." What's cool is that God blended one of my greatest loves—writing— with one of my greatest struggles—my singleness—and created something that's blessed my socks off.

Over the past year and a half I've written a lot about the single life (some of it included in the pages of this book) and heard from countless single people like you. One of the themes of the e-mails I've received about my column is the sentiment "You struggle with that too? I thought I was the only one. It's so nice to know I'm not alone!" As they say, misery loves company. But from these readers, I've also learned that joy, quirkiness, and celebration love company, too. I now know that a whole bunch of us struggle with whom to invite to the company Christmas party, sing and dance spontaneously when home alone, "try on" men's last names before the first date, and have lonely seasons and I-love-being-single seasons.

That's another main reason I wanted to write this book—to shed light on the fact that though at times we might be lonely, we're not alone. There are a bunch of us out here, bumbling our way through making the most of our singleness. When we open up and share the good, the bad, and the ugly parts of singleness with each other, we all benefit and move toward stronger, more savvy singleness. This book is a compilation of the lessons I've learned from chats with God, my single girlfriends, counseling sessions, readers of my singles column, and a whole bunch of trial and error. I pray it will send you on an amazing journey toward well-rounded, full-bodied singleness.

What If . . . ?

One of the best lessons I've learned in all my thinking, wrestling, and growing as a single woman is the danger of playing the "what if" game. *What if I missed the man I was supposed to marry? What if I never find the love of my life? What if I'd married Mr. Close Enough?* These questions rarely lead to anything productive, but, amazingly enough, when I was in the throes of writing this book, they did. Wallowing in self-doubt one day (I may be happy, but I'm still human!) and musing on the dubious honor of being a singles-book author (does that mean I'm an expert at singleness?), I toyed with the latter of these three questions. What if I had married my Mr. Close Enough? What if life had taken the course I'd expected—that I'd met Mr. Right in college, married shortly thereafter, and started making babies in my late twenties? As I pictured my life in that alternate universe, I wondered if I would have pursued my lifelong love of writing as early and with as much gusto. I thought back to the little girl I once was—attempting to become the youngest book author at age six (during my fascination with *The Guinness Book of World Records* phase!) and creating my own newsletter for my sixth-grade class—and wondered if that part of me would have gotten lost in wifehood and mommyhood.

What dreams would I have put on hold or given up altogether for that brand of success? What if, indeed.

So last year on Valentine's Day, instead of signing a gushy love letter to a soulmate, I signed a contract to write a singles book. And within weeks of turning thirty, instead of giving birth to a little bundle of joy, I birthed my first book manuscript. This is the life with which God has blessed me. Instead of questioning his timing or wisdom, I'm learning to celebrate each WooHoo moment with all the gusto I can muster.

Life may not have turned out the way I once thought it would. But I'm learning that sometimes this is a tremendous blessing.

So, Why Aren't You Married Yet?

S o, why aren't you married yet?"

If you're like me, you've been asked this question more times by more people than you can count. And if you're like me, you've wanted to bonk these Curious Georges and Georgettes on the head for asking such an insensitive, unanswerable question. Of course, there are variations on the query. "So what's a nice girl like you doing still single?" "When are you going to settle down and get married?" Or the slightly more subtle, "So are you married?" To which you answer, "No." And if the person doesn't follow up with "Why not?" you can almost hear the words running through his or her mind in the awkward silence that follows. And then there's the holiday version: "So when are you going to bring someone special home with you?" The bridal shower/wedding version: "So when is it going to be *your* turn?" And the grandparent-guilt version: "Do you think I'll see you get married—maybe even hold a grand-child or two—before I'm called home to heaven?"

Just when you want to run screaming from the dinner table, receiving line, airplane seat, or coffee-shop counter, you have to remind yourself that, really, most of these people are asking out of concern for your happiness. (If they only knew that *not* asking this question would make you so much happier!)

Single Stuff

All I Have
by Rita Springer

This dusky-voiced woman's lyrics of sold-out devotion and dependence on God give perspective on days when you feel like you're missing out. These touching praise songs are easy to sing along with and are great reminders that you already have all you need.

I'm not sure it's the nosi-ness factor that bothers me about this kind of question-ing as much as the underly-ing implication that there's a problem (we're single) that needs to be solved (by getting hitched, of course). And hidden deep behind the well-meaning intentions, concerned looks, and suggestions is a message that took me a long time to recognize and realize had infiltrated my thinking: There must be something wrong with me because I haven't gotten married yet.

I'll be the first to admit, there are some single people who are unmarried for, well, seemingly obvious reasons. The socially awkward, the painfully shy, the bowl-you-over brash people of this world sometimes take a while to find a life partner—and sometimes never do. It's tempting to point at these quirks—as well as our own—and deem singles unlovable and unmar-ryable. But when you think about it (and I mean nothing against married folk here), don't you know just as many awkward, shy, brash, annoying, passive, not-so-pretty, not-so-nice people who *are* married? (An old friend of mine used to put this very ineloquently: "There's a lid for every trash can!")

When we take a step back and look at the big picture, we real-ize there isn't something wrong with just us single people;

there's something wrong with *all* of us. Those who believe in a Savior and a world in need of saving should know this already. So why do we get swayed into thinking singles are especially flawed? Well, because in a world filled with the aforementioned questions asked by well-meaning people, love songs and romantic movies and sex-sells advertising, and grocery stores that stock nothing in a quantity less than family size, we single Christian women are misfits of sorts. But don't panic; it's not all bad and it's not unchangeable!

Misfits

As I'm sure you've noticed, our churches are extremely family oriented. There are sermons on being a good spouse and parent; Sunday school classes for newlyweds, parents of young children, parents of teens, and empty nesters; family potlucks and back-to-school ice cream socials; couples' retreats and father-daughter banquets. These are all wonderful things that definitely belong in the church. But I'm afraid our churches, in an effort to counteract the decay of the family unit in society, have almost overcompensated so that family equals church and church equals family. This sounds fine until you try to factor in singles. Where do we fit in on Sunday morning? Sadly, sometimes we're left to conclude that we don't. (We'll discuss this more in later chapters.)

Then you have the media. Last year single women were called the new "It Girl" in a *Time* magazine cover story, and Ally McBeal, Bridget Jones, and the women of *Friends* and *Sex and the City* are ambassadors of sorts for the growing number of single women in our society. When *Friends* first came on the air, I was so relieved to finally see *me* on my TV screen (albeit a funnier, richer, more beautiful version of me!). The show's actors not only popularized singleness, they made it seem cool. But as fun and liberating as it is to relate to some of these single women's frustrations and neurotic tendencies, as a Christian I can't relate to the way they find fulfillment in bed-, bar-, and mall-hopping. (And as a real human being, I can't relate to their size-two bodies!)

So that leaves us Christian single women stuck in the no-man's-land between *Sex and the City* and soccer mom, sort of relating to both camps but not really belonging in either. Add this misfit misfortune to our own Cinderella-inspired expectations, the dynamics of this paired-off world, and the nosy questions of friends, family, and strangers, and we're left feeling not only lonely, but alone.

It's My Pity Party . . .

I remember a time when the pain of this aloneness went so deep, it almost hurt physically. Five years ago I was sitting on a plane awaiting the takeoff of the return leg of a business trip, and though I'd just singlehandedly represented my company to numerous clients and conducted several successful interviews, I had tears in my eyes. Though I was surrounded by a sea of humanity on this sold-out flight, I felt utterly alone. And it was all the flight attendant's fault!

To be fair, she had no idea what she'd done. After the usual song and dance about what to do if the plane suddenly plummeted toward the earth, she interrupted the preflight silence with an extra announcement: "We are thrilled to have not one, not two, but *three* honeymooning couples on board with us today. We hope you newlyweds will enjoy a lifetime of happiness—as well as your complimentary beverages."

Great, I thought to myself in a moment of Gen-X cynicism, *not only do these people get lifetime partners, they also get free drinks!* Once again I felt like I was on the outside looking in on the rest of the happily paired-off world.

As I gazed out the window at the darkening sky, my spirits grew dim as well. In fact, I sank into a full-fledged pity party right there in seat 16-C. I thought about the couples launching into their new lives together—full of hope, wonder, and the security of having a lifetime companion. In contrast, when we landed I would be met by a stranger from the airport shuttle service who would deliver me to my empty apartment. In a couple of weeks I would be attending yet another wedding, and I still hadn't figured out who to take with me as my "and guest"— a far cry from even envisioning myself walking down the aisle with a soulmate.

As the plane gathered speed and finally lifted off the ground, a few tears escaped from the corners of my eyes. *That's never going to be me,* I thought as I pictured the honeymooners on board toasting this new journey—both literal and symbolic. *I'm never going to get married.* And then the universal single myth capped off my mental monologue: *There must be something wrong with me.*

Looking back, I realize how pathetic this whole scenario was. But in my conversations with countless single women, I've discovered scenarios like that are also very common. The type of situation may vary—the company Christmas party where everyone except you has a built-in significant other to bring, your high school reunion, Valentine's Day, Mother's Day, receiving five wedding invitations in one year (all from women younger than you), going to a romantic movie with The Girls instead of a date, not being able to find a non-love song on your car radio, watching married women be dropped off at the door of the mall while you drive around in the rain to find a parking place, sitting in a sea of couples and families at church on Sunday morning. But whatever the cause, the resulting feeling is the same.

So, Why Aren't We Married Yet?

How can we rid ourselves of the feeling that something is wrong with us simply because we're not married? Well, how about exploring the fact that when confronted by the question

"Why aren't you married yet?" we automatically jump to negative responses. What about the positives? What about the fact that we refuse to settle for less than God's best for us? Or that we want to find a great father for our future children? We're still milking the great things about being single. We're still figuring out who we are and want to sort out "me" before becoming a "we." We don't want to get married just because everyone else is (I mean, everyone else is wearing shorty-shorts and halter tops and listening to Britney Spears, too!). We don't want just a warm body; we want a lifetime love, and that sometimes takes a while to find. We don't take "'til death do us part" lightly and don't want to risk becoming a divorce statistic. We have work and ministry options we'd like to explore first. We're simply not ready yet, or if we are, we simply haven't found Mr. Right.

I'm not sure how or when marriage became the mark of an "okay" human being, or, more important, how we singles accepted it as the mark of an okay human being. When I started looking at how I'd allowed myself to be lulled into this thinking, I saw subtle yet flawed reasons, many of which surprised me and most of which vanished when I brought them to light. For example, there was the belief that I was only "lovable" if I found someone who would pledge to be with me 'til death do us part. However, in seeking this stamp of approval, many married people have made hasty or unwise choices in their path to the altar, which only seems to underscore what a silly guideline this is. Of course, there's also the majority-rule argument—the concept that most people are married and that those of us who aren't are left behind because we're somehow inferior. But when has simply being in the minority ever made someone wrong? It's like I'd somehow degenerated to the "logic" of junior high, when I got that feathered haircut all the "cool" girls had just so I'd be counted among them. The results of this kind of thinking weren't pretty then, and they aren't pretty now.

Just like getting your hair cut, getting married is easy. More than two million people do it every year. Sadly, we've all heard the depressing stats about how many of those marriages stick.

What baffles me is that those of us who are "still single" seem to be given a harder time as we hold out for a right, one-time-only marriage. We don't just want a marriage; we want a fulfilling, God-honoring life—whatever that may look like. That's the more difficult—though much more rewarding—path. And frankly, that's the path we deserve, the one Jesus spoke of when he said he came to this earth (from the glory of heaven, no less) to give us abundant life. I don't know about you, but I like the thought of an abundant life—much more so than a cookie-cutter kind of existence. And though it scared me to death, it wasn't until I was willing to embrace my singleness and dive whole-hog into this phase of life—not knowing if it would be five months, five years, five decades, or forever—that I finally discovered a truly happy, abundant life.

But I'm getting ahead of myself. First we need to get past this we-must-be-flawed-because-we're-still-single deception. Check out the next chapter for a few perspective-changing tactics I've discovered.

Antidotes for the Single Girl Blues

*L*et me take you back again to my traumatic plane ride. I was embarrassed by losing it that day, so I quickly tried to pull myself together before the woman sitting in 16-B felt the need for an intervention. In an effort to stop the waterworks, I accidentally stumbled onto one of the best things I've found for putting a wet blanket on a pity party: Picture a friend in your shoes and think of what you'd say to console her.

As I started flipping through the in-flight magazine to divert my attention, I also began a mental lecture: *Okay now, Camerin, let's be real here. Never? Never get married? You're a smart person; you know that "nevers" are rarely true. Don't the stats say that only like 10 percent of the population never get married? So that means most likely you'll get hitched eventually. You just haven't met the right person yet. And you definitely don't want to settle and risk becoming a miserable married or a divorce statistic. It's not like this whole marriage thing is a race anyway. So, relax and enjoy the view already.*

My counselor calls this self-talk. My Bible calls this thinking about things that are true (Phil. 4:8). I call it my salvation on days when singleness stinks. So what do you hear when you tune in to the voice in your head? Is it positive? Is it true? If your mental monologue is making you miserable, become your own best friend and give yourself a kindhearted talking to. (Or if that's too difficult, pour your heart out to a trusted single gal pal and let her give the loving lecture.) If you (or she) need some ammo, check out these reassuring single stats from the U.S. Census Bureau:

- People who wait until their thirties to marry experience a much lower divorce rate.
- Athough married men are reported to be happier than single men, single women are reported to be happier than married women.
- From 1970 to 1999, the percentage of adults who lived alone increased from 8 percent to 13 percent.
- Between 1970 and 1998, the percentage of females aged 25–29 who have never been married has risen from 19.1 percent to 38.6 percent, and the percentage of females aged 30–34 who have never been married has risen from 9.4 percent to 21.6 percent.
- The median ages for first marriages have risen considerably in recent decades and are at an all-time high in American history: 25 for women and 27 for men.

Twenty-Five Great Things about Claire

A couple years ago my friend Claire and I were sipping mochas in our favorite coffee shop hangout when she told me something I found utterly disturbing. Apparently her counselor, whom she'd been seeing for a while to help her sort out some family issues, had given her an assignment to write a list of twenty-five great things about herself. The shocker was that smart, funny, professional, godly Claire could barely come up with nine.

I stared at her in disbelief for a few moments before I started naming possible additions to her list. "What about your great sense of humor?" I said, recalling giggle fests over everything from funny movies to faux pas.

"I'm not that funny. And humor isn't really a 'great' quality, is it?" she said meekly.

"What about your kind heart? You're always willing to help others, and you give really cool and thoughtful gifts," I suggested, remembering her offers of rides to and from the airport and the "I'd Rather Be in Paris" pillow she'd given me the previous Christmas.

She paused a moment, then dismissed my efforts with, "You're just being nice."

I could tell I was getting nowhere, so I changed the subject, we continued chatting, and eventually we parted ways. I was still troubled, however, so I determined to help my friend see herself through different eyes. I think that's one of the reasons why God gave us the body of Christ, families, and friends—to remind us of the wonderful ways he's wired each of us and to point us to our Maker, who loves us more than we can fathom.

Later that afternoon, God dropped a great idea in my head, and in a rare moment of follow-through I began crafting an e-mail entitled "Twenty-Five Awesome Things about Claire." *She can't argue with an e-mail,* I reasoned. So I breathed a prayer: "God, you know and care about Claire so much more than I do; please help me write this list."

Together, God and I came up with qualities as whimsical as "Claire's so fun she bought her pet cat a pet fish" and as serious as "She has a deep desire to be a godly woman." I finally got to Awesome Thing Number Twenty-Five—"Claire's fearfully and wonderfully made" (Ps. 139:14)—then clicked send.

Several hours later I received a call from Claire. "That's the nicest thing anyone's ever done for me," were the first words out of her mouth. She was obviously moved. And I was, too, when she told me that she and her sister had just memorized Psalm 139:14.

"I got goosebumps when I saw that you'd mentioned that verse as the last point on your list," she said. "How did you know?"

"To be honest, I can't take any credit. That was God's idea," I said, marveling that the Creator of the universe took the time to remind Claire—and me—that we're awesome children of an awesome God.

Your mission, should you choose to accept it, is to write a list of twenty-five great qualities about *you.* If you have trouble, enlist the help of friends, family, and most important, the One who made you great. Once you've made a list of great things about you, why not do the same for a single friend of yours who needs a confidence boost? She'll be encouraged, and you may just get blessed in the process, too.

If you question the scriptural soundness of this assignment—what about humility and the verse that says "Do not think of yourself more highly than you ought" (Rom. 12:3)?—I respectfully challenge you to look up the word "love" in a concordance and start reading through the numerous Bible verses that affirm how much your Creator loves and values you. I'm not suggesting you trot around with I'm-all-that haughtiness, but I am suggesting that thinking too lowly of yourself—even hating yourself—is just as sinful. You are a creation of the Most High God, who crafted you in your mother's womb (Ps. 139:13), who engraved you on the palms of his hands (Isa. 49:16), and who loved you enough—even before you were born—to send his Son to die in your place for your sins. When you think *too* lowly of yourself, you discredit all that—and you dishonor God.

Let Your Married Friends Be Your Guide

One day during that midafternoon slump when intelligent thoughts are hard to come by, several of my coworkers and I were standing around chatting. Somehow the conversation turned to my recent trip to Germany to visit a good friend of mine whose husband is stationed there in the air force. As my married and mom-type coworkers practically salivated at my ability to just pick up and go, I smiled at the chance to be the one with the coveted life for once. Not that I condone coveting—it's just that usually I'm the one listening to all of them talk about their spouse and offspring and thinking wistful thoughts. How cool to finally be the one with the great life!

As the conversation broke up and we returned to our respective cubicles, Carla, one of those great, tell-it-like-it-is women who works down the hall from me, said something I still treasure: "You know, you often remind me of the things I miss most about being single. I think it's great you're taking advantage of this time in your life."

Single Stuff

The Missing Piece Meets the Big 0
by Shel Silverstein

"Just say 'no' to codependency" in a charmingly childlike story. See what a healthy relationship between two *whole* people looks like.

Her comments introduced a new thought to me. Could there really be enough great things about being single that married women would trade in their perks for ours? I knew it worked the other way around, that single women often long for the companionship, security, procreation possibilities (and practice!), and love and affirmation married women enjoy, as well as the presence of a soulmate on whom to lavish our love and affirmation. Even when we're enlightened enough to know married life isn't all romance, there are countless days we'd be happy to take on the drawbacks in order to get the good stuff. But are there really times when married women would take on the loneliness, nosy relatives, and odd-one-out feelings of singleness to get to the good stuff of our life station?

I had to ask. "What do you miss most about being single?"

Carla thought for a moment, then said, "Oh, you know, the closeness you have to your girlfriends. The freedom you have to go out to eat with your friends . . . on the spur of the moment . . . and on a weeknight. And without having to get a sitter! The ability you have to travel, to take swing-dance lessons (my husband is *not* interested), and to buy a fifth pair of black shoes without needing to explain or justify that necessity to anyone."

We both laughed at the shared understanding of this latter phenomenon, then I thanked Carla for reminding me how good I have it. As I walked back to my office, I realized that though I'd taken advantage of all these perks of singleness, I hadn't truly appreciated them. Although some of them seemed trivial, if they were to suddenly depart from my life, I knew I'd miss them. Once again, I'd accidentally stumbled onto a great exercise to promote happier singlehood.

So I started asking a few of my trusted married friends what they missed most about their single days. Now, some of them never were truly single, having married right out of high school or college, and some were so completely entrenched in wedded bliss that they couldn't answer my question. But some of these women, especially those who'd married a little later in life, offered great insights. I made mental notes of their answers and resolved to appreciate— or take advantage of, if I wasn't already—the perks of singleness they'd valued and now missed.

If you've got married friends, let the inquiry begin. (If you don't, you really need some—for this and other reasons we'll get into in a later chapter.)

Celebrate Your Singleness!

Okay, now it's time to put into practice all this great new info about great single you. Here's what I suggest: Treat yourself once a week; attack another dream once a year.

Treat Yourself

With others questioning your singleness and no one man signed up to affirm you, you need to take time to pamper yourself and remind yourself that you rock—regardless of your marital status. So, figure out what makes you happy, how God has gifted you, where you most enjoy serving others, and what perk of singleness you like best. Play up these positives in little ways once a week. I enjoy a leisurely lunch hour (after munching lunch at my desk while working) at the local Starbuck's with a Mocha Frappuccino and a great travel narrative. It rejuvenates me, juices me up for an afternoon in the office, and inspires hopes and ideas that have nothing to do with a man. Which leads to my next point . . .

Attack Another Dream

There are so many other goals you can have control of in your life right now—learning a foreign language, taking a photography class, sponsoring a child overseas, mastering basic home improvement skills. Focus on those things you can control instead of that one elusive thing you can't. It's empowering, especially when you feel powerless to fulfill your desire for a mate or to make that ache go away. It broadens you as a person and gives you even more to offer Mr. Right if he ever does decide to grace the scene. It makes you more attractive—there's nothing more compelling than someone doing something she loves. And it gives God other ways to bless and use you. What could be more abundant than that?

The idea is to create such a great single life that you don't notice who's "missing," that you wouldn't dare let anything less than God's best pry you away from it, and that you experience God's presence and purpose in your life as they were meant to be experienced—individually and unconditionally. And to get to the place where the next time someone asks, "What's a nice girl like you doing still single?" you can answer: "Having the time of my life!"

Singleness and Scripture

Something my single friend Cathy said recently sent me to my Bible with furrowed brow. We were chatting with some other single Christian girlfriends about our single state when Cathy voiced her frustration with verses such as Proverbs 5:18: "May your fountain be blessed, and may you rejoice in the wife of your youth." It was the word "youth" that had this thirtysomething a bit dismayed. "At the rate I'm going, I'm not going to be anyone's wife, let alone the wife of someone's youth," she said, half joking and half serious. Then she asked a troubling question: "What do we single women do with verses such as these?"

Martha! Martha! Martha!

I thought of the woman described in Proverbs 31, the Martha Stewart of the Bible whom so many of us aspire to be. I love that she has such varied talents and pursuits and seems like a strong, capable woman, but I looked at the fact that she's married with kids and wondered how much of this is just description of one particular godly woman and how much of this is prescription of what godly women *should* look like. Then I thought of the oft-quoted-to-singles verse, "Your Maker is your husband" (Isa. 54:5), which feels both comforting and like a platitude all at the same time. Even though this verse is part of a larger metaphor referring to God's future relationship with Jerusalem, the sentiment that God is with us always—especially in the absence of a husband—is totally in keeping with the rest of the Bible. And while that truth can be a lifesaver on the lonely days of singleness, there are moments, I have to admit, when it feels like a booby prize. I mean, God's with *all* of us, married and single. So single women get God's presence all the time, while married women get God's presence all the time *and* the physical presence of a husband to hold hands with, hug, and do all kinds of other stuff that sounds so great and seemed so lacking in my life.

Realizing how selfish and shallow I was beginning to sound, I turned to my Bible in search of answers. As I was thumbing through the back of my study Bible, I stumbled on something tucked between the concordance and map index that I'd never noticed before: a subject index. *Huh.* I looked up singleness and, lo and behold, "single" was there. I was encouraged by this newly discovered list. That is, until I looked up the first verse, Proverbs 18:22: "He who finds a wife finds what is good and receives favor from the LORD." *Great.* The next one was even worse. Isaiah 4:1 reads, "In that day seven women will take hold of one man and say, 'We will eat our own food and provide our own clothes; only let us be called by your name. Take away our disgrace!'" The seven-to-one ratio sounded familiar from my years in church singles groups, and I was suddenly really curious about God's stance on singles. Was the s-i-n at the beginning of the word there for a reason? And if so, what exactly have we singles done to deserve this harsh view of us?

The next verse listed was a command for the Old Testament prophet Jeremiah: "You must not marry and have sons or daughters in this place" (Jer. 16:2). This was just as perplexing as the previous verses until I read a bit of context and the study notes in the margin, which suggested God was saving Jeremiah from heartbreak, since the next generation would suffer disease, war, and famine, or possibly was preserving his single-minded devotion to God's huge call on his life. This latter point jived with the rest of the verses listed under "single" in my Bible's subject index—Matthew 19:11–12 and 1 Corinthians 7:28, 34—which all spoke of the blessing of a heart undivided and undistracted from devotion to God. The passage in 1 Corinthians 7:34 seemed to sum it up best: "An unmarried woman or virgin is concerned about the Lord's affairs: Her aim is to be devoted to the Lord in both body and spirit. But a married woman is concerned about the affairs of this world—how she can please her husband." Earlier in this passage, verse 28 goes so far as to say, "Those who marry will face many troubles in this life, and I want to spare you this." And in verse 1 of this chapter, Paul even says it is good not to marry.

Hopelessly Devoted to You

Paul himself is like the poster child for the merits of the single life. His words in one of his letters to the Corinthians, "It is good for a man not to marry" (1 Cor. 7:1), have inspired both sighs of relief and shudders of fear in Christian singles everywhere. While we like the defense of the single life, we wonder at the permanency of the comment. Does he mean it's good for a person not to marry . . . *ever?* While I venture his answer to that question is yes, I think he's stating a truth more than a prescription. In fact, later in this passage Paul says, "I am saying this for your own good, not to restrict you, but that you may live in a right way in undivided devotion to the Lord" (1 Cor.7:35).

Devotion to the Lord. Isn't that what all Christians are called to? In the Old Testament, the prophet Micah spells out what God requires of us: "To act justly and to love mercy and to walk humbly with your God" (Micah 6:8). Jesus' last words while he walked in human form on this earth were a reminder to his disciples of their primary purpose: to be his witnesses to the ends of the earth. Micah didn't tell us to pair off and attend as many church family potlucks as possible. Jesus didn't instruct us to search the ends of the earth for a soulmate. Our mission as mysterious creations of the ultimate Creator is to live for him. That's it—whether we're single, hitched, young, in our Oil of Olay years, a parent of a preschooler, childless, willowy, wide, rolling in dough, or strapped for cash. And Paul's point in 1 Corinthians 7 is one we shouldn't take lightly or skim over (either accidently or purposely out of fear): We singles are more free to passionately pursue our main purpose on this earth. And while this truth might not seem like much at the end of the day when we're craving a hand to hold and a heart to call our own, at the end of all time, when all is said and done, it will have been a privilege, not a booby prize, to have had fewer distractions standing between us and the Author of life, the Creator of the universe, the Lover of our souls.

Single Stuff

"At Last" by Etta James

This is why we aren't settling for just any ol' husband. I want this song played at my wedding reception (that's the only part I have planned, really!). And while it plays, I want to be dancing with someone I can truly sing this about, someone worth waiting for. Etta's soaring, emotive vocals make me all dreamy every time they play this at my neighborhood Starbuck's. *Sigh.*

A few weeks after my Bible verse search, I found myself at a conference chatting with a woman who'd married at eighteen and was the mom of three kids. She was thrilled to be away from home to get "five minutes of quiet time" to herself. In the usual course of small talk, we ended up doing a friendly comparison of our lives. She told me about how unromantic having a husband can be—"They come with all kinds of smells and sounds you wouldn't believe!" she said, laughing, I suspect, at memories supporting the veracity of this comment. She talked about the constant demands her three kids put on her daily routine. I talked of my silent apartment and the fact that a couple of my closest friendships exist almost solely over the phone. But as she brought up how much she loves her kids and big lug of a husband, I talked about how great it is to be able to just chat aloud with God while washing my dishes or to listen to praise music really loud while getting ready for work in the mornings. I thought of the church committee I'm on and how much more I've been able to volunteer for tasks big and small than the moms in the bunch. And I thought of my friend Susan, whose marriage is on the brink of divorce, and how she'd recently expressed how much she appreciates that, unlike her married friends and family members, I'm available practically anytime she needs some spur-of-the-moment support.

So I began to wonder what my life would look like if I really did use my singleness to give more undivided devotion to God. Not because I have to—because it's really easy for us singles to serve God and the church out of duty or guilt, since we know we've got more time and energy to offer—but out of pure joy and love for God. What would my life look like if I used this season, be it short or long, to allow God to become my first and best love, instead of wasting that extra energy on whining, pining, and mining the man-field out there for Mr. Right?

I don't have the answer to this question yet, because this is a new revelation, a new quest. I've been praying a lot recently for God to help me reinvest the energy I expend noticing single men (through the ever-so-subtle ring check) and wondering if they're noticing me . . . and if we'll end up dating . . . and if we'll share the story of how we met with our grandchildren (don't laugh, you know you do this too!). I've been praying that instead I'll have that kind of finely tuned radar for God's presence and fingerprints. How rich would life be if we were constantly on the lookout for God instead of Mr. Right? I suspect it would be kind of like having a love affair with God.

We have some great things on which to base this quest. The best promises in the Bible come packaged for anyone, not just couples. "God so loved the world that he gave his one and only Son, that *whoever* believes in him shall not perish but have eternal life" (John 3:16, italics mine), and each of us—regardless of our marital status—are "fearfully and wonderfully made" (Ps. 139:14). I'm grateful that another one of my favorite verses, Zephaniah 3:17—"The LORD your God is with you, he is mighty to save. He will take great delight in you, he will quiet you with his love, he will rejoice over you with singing"—doesn't come with any conditions or marital prerequisites. While the Proverbs 31 woman was called blessed by her children, was praised by her husband, and is often touted in churches today, we also have to look at seemingly single New Testament sisters Martha and Mary, who were personal friends of Jesus and witnessed some of his most amazing miracles (including the raising of their brother, Lazarus, from the dead). And I agree with the apostle Paul in Romans 8:38–39 when he says, "For I am convinced that neither death nor life, neither angels nor demons, neither the present nor the future, nor any powers, neither height nor depth, nor anything else in all creation, will be able to separate us from the love of God that is in Christ Jesus our Lord." I would add that nosy relatives, confusing verses, frustrations and lonely days, insensitive comments about our singleness, and feelings of being left out by the church can't separate us from his love either. That is, unless we allow them to. And what a tragedy that would be.

We singles may not have vows from a husband, but we have promises from the Creator of the universe. And if that's not enough for us now, it's never going to be enough, and we won't find the kind of true joy we often erroneously seek in the arms of a mortal man. So let the love affair begin!

Solo on Sunday Morning

I hate to admit it, but sometimes Sunday morning is the loneliest part of my week. I often sit by myself—which is partly my own fault since my friends and I can never seem to coordinate when we're in town, which of our church's three services to attend, and in which section of the large sanctuary to look for each other. Then again, if I were attending with my family, this wouldn't be an issue at all. So I sit there in a sea of happy couples and families, with empty chairs on either side of me, feeling like I'm in a deodorant commercial (cue the TV announcer: "Why is no one sitting by YOU?!"). My friend Kathryn recently told me about a church service she got nearly nothing out of because from her vantage point she could barely see the pastor between the heads of the couple constantly chatting and exchanging loving glances in the row directly in front of her. The distraction was both literal and symbolic, as she didn't even have *anyone* sitting next to her with whom to chat if she'd wanted to, let alone a spouse, like everyone else in the sanctuary seemed to have.

But seating logistics are just the tip of the iceberg. Two summers ago, my church ran a four-week sermon series on marriage. Four weeks! I attended each week and really did attempt to get something out of the sermons—and to his credit, my pastor tried to make the info accessible and helpful to people of all walks of life. But there's only so much knowledge you can apply to your own situation and that you can tuck away for future use. And I couldn't help but think that the church has never run even a one-time sermon on singleness—that would seem somehow odd and misplaced. I love my pastor; he's a wonderfully gifted teacher whose sermons possess a rare blend of appeal to both head and heart. But, like most pastors in America, the lion's share of his anecdotes and advice revolves around spouses or school—leaving me, who's neither a wife nor a student, feeling invisible.

In my church, as I'm sure is true in many churches, communion is served by the elders . . . often accompanied by their wives. This makes sense on some logistical levels, but it also leaves me with a few perplexing questions: How does being married to an elder make one more qualified to serve? Is their wife's spiritual condition part of the criteria for these men to become elders? Why aren't there any single elders in my church? Will I be able to serve in this capacity only if I get married—and to someone with elder-potential? It's not that I'm fixated on serving communion, I just think this whole structure leaves out some prime people—namely, singles—to serve in the church.

Years ago I was new to the area I'm in now, and I visited several local churches in search of a body of believers to call home. On one particular Sunday, the church-of-the-week's sermon was about forgiveness in marriage, and near the end of the service the pastor asked the married couples in the sanctuary to turn to each other and repeat his words asking for forgiveness and then receiving it from each other. While it was incredibly moving to watch these emotional, often tearful exchanges, and while I wholeheartedly believe in healthy, God-honoring marriage, I again felt like the odd one out—this time not even sure where to direct my attention in this room full of private couple moments.

I don't mean to bash the church. It's difficult to even speak badly about it. I love the church. I *am* the church. But there are times when I feel more like its black-sheep spinster aunt than one of its valued daughters. And this makes me sad on many levels—for feeling like I don't belong in the house of the One who created unconditional love and acceptance, for the singles who have left the church entirely because it's simply too painful to be there, for the singles who don't yet know Jesus and will be that much more difficult to attract to a body of believers, and for younger generations who are getting a distorted and unbalanced image of what the body of Christ should be.

Time for a Change?

I admit there have been times when I've become the Official Complainer of the Singles Perspective, when I've seemed to always be grousing about something the church wasn't doing right for singles. After a while I knew I was doing more harm than good (making people equate "singles" with "oh, no, here we go again!"), and my few good points fell on deaf ears (because people just heard whining). I learned the hard way that people are most receptive to suggestions for change when they're delivered with kindness and in the context of a well-rounded, give-and-take relationship. We've got to be open to others' perspectives if we want them to be open to ours.

It wasn't until I joined a committee at my church a couple years ago and began to forge these kinds of positive relationships that I started to make a difference for singles in my church. And in the process I learned an important lesson: A lot of the movers and shakers in the church have no idea there's a problem for those of us who are single. The next logical conclusion was equally important and called for action: How can we expect things to change if no one knows things need changing? The solution I stumbled on involved running in the right circles and simply voicing the single perspective—lovingly and in moderation, of course (more on this in the next chapter).

Single Stuff

Mansfield Park

You think marrying well is difficult now? Try adding the pressures of class, family, and financial security the women in this lesser-known Jane Austen flick/book had to deal with. Fanny Price, our strong, single female protagonist of humble beginnings, exemplifies the absolute beauty and honor of following your heart and refusing to settle. Rumored to be Austen's favorite of her own stories.

Sometimes being a mouthpiece isn't enough, and we need to put some walk with our talk. My friend Julie is a great example of this. At a church she used to attend, there was no singles group, but she and her friends felt the need for one and knew of other singles in the church who also longed for this kind of ministry. So instead of just complaining, Julie and a handful of her friends helped start a singles group. They worked with the church to find out what was required to make this ministry happen, then dove in and provided the structure, leadership, and work needed to get the group off the ground. Within months they had a singles Sunday school class in full swing, and within a year they had the telltale sign of any successful ministry: committees! Another single I know who launched and helps run the singles ministry in her church talked about how attitude is everything. "If I have a 'poor me' attitude and wait for others to come to me, then people ignore me or treat me like a 'poor you.' One of the keys to the success of our singles ministry is that we don't sit around and wait for things to happen; we go make them happen."

Stop and ask yourself some questions: Are my words making a positive or negative impression for singles in my church? Am I willing to put some walk with my talk? What do I wish my church was doing differently in regards to singles? And even more important, are there any steps—large or small— I can take to help create this change? Got your answers? Now prayerfully make the changes you feel God is calling you to— in yourself or in your church.

Consider the Source

After years of feeling left out and fielding insensitive comments because of my singleness—and not wanting this to turn me into a bitter woman with an axe to grind, especially in the context of the church—I've learned the importance of looking at the heart of the "offender." Usually the wounding words are uttered out of ignorance, loving concern for our welfare, or issues within the utterer in regard to his or her own life station. And these words are often perceived as offensive because of our own issues and hang-ups. I remember one incident that was sort of a cross between these two reasons and was, oddly enough, resolved by a one-year-old.

It all started when Diana, the nursery guru for the toddler class at my church, asked me if I had any kids. I was a substitute for the nursery, a position I'd volunteered for so I could snuggle with all the cute little people I'd spied in the church lobby over the past couple years.

It was Diana's attention to detail that made her question about my parenthood status such a surprise. She seemed to have all eight babies in the room on her mental radar screen at once. She'd dashed to save Jennifer, who'd crawled dangerously close to the rocking chair legs, and Steven, who'd wedged himself behind a bouncy chair in his quest for a wayward ball, before I'd even noticed these little cuties had escaped from the pack.

With such a finely tuned radar, couldn't she sense my amateur status around the kiddies? And couldn't she see I wasn't wearing a wedding ring? This was her first attempt at any sort of personal conversation, so I politely responded, "Nope. I'm single. I mean, I know you can be single and have kids, but I don't have any." There I was, explaining away my singleness again—and oh-so-awkwardly. A wailing baby saved her from having to find some sort of appropriate response.

A few seconds later Diana launched into a conversation with Susan, the other nursery worker, about their own babies, their husbands, and, as seemingly all women who've been through childbirth eventually discuss, their labor stories. I listened and asked questions about their respective families, wondering if I would ever graduate from passive listener to active participant in these all-important, ever-recurring Grown-up Women Conversations. As usual, I wished the conversation would shift to summer plans or faith or work or anything else to which I could contribute.

About ten minutes later, Diana tried again. "So are you a college student?" she asked. I felt like she was trying to figure out why I wasn't a wife and mom. For some reason I felt the need to justify my existence with a quick rundown of my resume; I'd been a fairly competent member of the corporate jungle for a good decade now. But I tempered my defensiveness and simply responded, "No, I'm a working person."

"Well," Diana responded, "Susan and I are both stay-at-home moms, and it's the best job in the whole world." They exchanged knowing smiles and started a new Grown-up Women Conversation about potty-training and homeschooling. Suddenly I felt like they were the insiders and I was the outsider, so out of place in the sea of primary-colored toys and squirming babies. I could tell they didn't even realize they'd just highly praised a position to which I couldn't even "apply," given my current marital status, and that absolutely everything they'd discussed was mom- and wife-oriented, leaving single childless me in the dust.

As I sat there, rattle in hand, feeling devalued and wanting to defend my singleness, I glanced over at little Christopher. He was the only walker in our bunch and definitely the most independent. He'd spent the morning happily exploring all the toys in the well-stocked room. At the moment, he was examining a plastic phone while slowly walking backwards. He was so captivated by the toy, he failed to notice little Jonathan behind him. Before I could move, there was a sprawling pile of little boys. In one of those beauty-of-toddlerhood moments—where spills that look like near-death experiences are shrugged off and forgotten—the two boys simply exchanged smiles, and each went back to his toy of choice.

There was a moment of stillness after that in which I sensed God faintly whispering, *Did you catch that?* He seemed to be showing me that sometimes in our individual pursuits of happiness and fulfillment, we clumsy humans trip over each other. Like Diana and her quest to be a God-honoring mom-with-a-capital-M, and me and my quest to be a respected single professional. We'd just tripped over each other, so to speak, and I had the choice to shake it off, as Christopher and Jonathan had, or to pitch a fit like a two-year-old terror. Diana didn't mean to be hurtful and exclusive. And I didn't need to be so defensive. I decided to follow the boys' example—and God's advice—and let it go.

I looked over at Diana, who was now playing peekaboo with a fussy little girl. Susan was nearby changing yet another diaper. As my bitterness melted, I realized afresh it's not us and them, marrieds and nonmarrieds, parents and nonparents. It's simply a collective us—children of God.

In a burst of warm fuzzy feelings, I scooped up Christopher in a big bear hug. "Thanks, " I whispered in his ear. Then I looked up and whispered another thanks to the Father of us all.

Singles Groupies
and Dropouts

*A*nyone who's spent time in a church singles group knows that they have the potential to be fabulous—or a big flop. Here are a few lessons I've learned from my own experiences in this perplexing gathering of people.

Singles Groups Are NOT Created Equal—
And They Aren't for Everyone

The first singles group I ever belonged to was awesome. Our leader was Pastor Janie, a woman with a big heart for singles— and just a big heart, period. I was in college at the time, and I loved that she regularly scheduled Sunday dinners in the homes of families within the church for those of us who were students. Homemade food was never more appreciated than by us normally cafeteria-bound college students. We devoured the food—and the family-oriented love and attention. Since most of us were displaced from our out-of-state families, these meals helped us feel like valued members of the body of believers. The singles group also met regularly for Bible studies, social events, and worship nights. After one fancy dinner out, we all went bowling in our dresses and shirts and ties, yukking it up and snapping photos of our unique fashion statements—complete with bowling shoes! We were a community, a family, a successful singles group.

After college, when I moved away from that area, I figured I could easily find another thriving singles group to join at whatever church I landed in. I had no idea what a tall order that was! At one medium-sized church, the singles group met (and fit comfortably, I might add) in the pastor's office. All eight of us—an eclectic bunch at best—shared an awkward, forgettable, silent-pause-filled discussion led by a married man in the congregation. I left the group, depressed by my singleness and the . . . um, *unique* selection of peers (and, let's be honest, dating possibilities!) I was beginning to fear would be my only option at church after church.

The next singles group I recall attending (several of the churches I checked out didn't have one, and I'll admit I chickened out of going to a few others after peeking in the room at the small or stilted gathering) was much larger and more social. I was the first one in the class—and the only one there for a good ten minutes (I assumed the regulars were mixing and mingling in the lobby after the service). I was about to bail when a guy finally wandered in the room and asked if I was looking for the college class. *Sigh.* (I keep telling myself that looking young for my age will *someday* be a blessing.) After I assured him I was in the right place, we chatted a bit. Everyone else finally wandered in, and we all enjoyed a thought-provoking discussion led by one of the guys in the class. Afterward I was impressed by how many people came up and introduced themselves to me. That is, until I realized they were all male. While I was flattered, I also had the sneaking suspicion I was fresh meat! This was confirmed in the weeks that followed when the attention turned from me to another new unattached female in the class. Ew!

With that experience in mind, I was especially impressed by the singles class at my current church. No meat-market feel—yea! Then again, there wasn't much of a friendly feel at all. It took a whopping six months before anyone in the class invited me to their weekly after-church lunch. Every week I sat there trying my best to look friendly, approachable, *breathing*, hoping someone would notice me. But the cliques continued, the conversations were almost always initiated by me, and after a year I finally called it quits. The church was great—I was fed, challenged, led into God's presence—but the singles group left me feeling frustrated and lonely, emotions I didn't want associated with my Sunday morning worship experience.

Single Stuff

*www.samresources
.com*

Home of singles ministry resources and conferences from Cook Communications. This site's especially helpful if you're trying to launch or maintain a singles ministry in your church.

At first I felt guilty for leaving. Did that mean I was running away from the problem? Did God want me to stay and help make the atmosphere more engaging for new people? Was I being selfish, picking and choosing the parts of the church that did and didn't work for me? I wrestled with these questions until I got involved in another ministry within the church and eventually made friends with a few of the people in the singles class (ironically, only after I left the class).

In the end, I realized that we need different things at different times during our Christian life. There have been seasons when I've needed a singles ministry, and times when I didn't (such as now, when I have a circle of single Christian friends who meet my needs for that kind of peer). I learned that there are a lot of meat-markety and oddball-rich singles groups out there—and sometimes we're called to be part of them, to help change what needs to be changed and to revel in some of the absurdity of it all. Other times it's better for everyone involved if we walk away. Attending a singles group isn't mandatory for godly singles; it doesn't earn us points in heaven. And if we stay there, miserable, out of a sense of duty, we'll only taint the group as well as our church experience. However, I think the walking away should be done with prayer and peace, not a "good riddance!" hollered over our shoulder as we run away.

So I've learned that, just as with churches, perfect singles groups don't exist—mainly because they're filled with us flawed human beings (flawed because we're human, not because we're single). And sometimes I think they don't exist because the singles-group model isn't necessarily the way the church was intended to operate. Because . . .

We Singles Shouldn't Be Sequestered and Sulking

I've heard several singles talk about the fact that their singles group often degenerates into a group gripe session about all the challenges of going solo. They sit in some basement room complaining about the fact that no one else in the church seems to include them or even acknowledge there are singles in the church. I know you're smart and can see this one a mile away: No one includes or acknowledges them because they can't be found. And even if they could, would you want to reach out to a group of people sporting pouts and snarls?

To be fair, it should be pointed out that this is an across-the-board "problem." During the Sunday school hour, the soon-to-be-marrieds are in one classroom, the newlyweds are in another, the parents of youngsters are down the hall next to the frazzled parents of teens and the "senior saints." While it makes sense that we group according to our similar life challenges and

needs, it's amazing how segregated we are on Sunday mornings. When you step back and take a discerning look at this
structure, it's difficult to see how it fits into the biblical description of the body of Christ. The situation almost sounds like the
childhood game of Cooties—heads over here, ears over there,
legs and noses scattered, nothing joining together to resemble
any sort of cohesive creature.

It wasn't until I opted out of the singles class and joined the
one topical class my church was offering, on spiritual gifts, that
I realized what I'd been missing in all my singles groups. There,
joined by a young couple with a baby, two other single friends,
an older, empty-nest couple, and the rest of a mixed bag of people from all corners of my church, I learned a lot from the class
curriculum . . . *and* from the interactions with this diverse
bunch. We all lent different perspectives as we sought to
uncover our respective spiritual gifts, and it was so rich to iden-
tify elbows, feet, and mouths in the body of Christ in the context in which we're supposed to operate—as a whole Cootie, so
to speak.

I love the e-mail I received from Christen, a reader of the singles column I write. She told me about being THE single person at her small church. Instead of feeling singled out, however, she took joy in playing with the numerous children in the
family-filled congregation. "All of these families would welcome me to their house on almost any Sunday after church,
indicating there's always room for one more," she wrote. Christen hosted a women's retreat at her house because she was cen-
trally located . . . and because there were no other people at her
house to bother. She's even been invited to attend the church's
annual Valentine's Day dinner right alongside all the couples.
"My church treats me no differently because I'm single, and
actually constantly reassures me I'm welcome there any time,"
she wrote. "I think that's what real Christianity looks like."
Amen.

I'm not saying a church singles group can't ever function as
a healthy, well-balanced body of Christ. But I do think there are

seasons of life when we need to belong to different kinds of communities—sometimes single, sometimes vastly different, sometimes a combo of everything in between. And when most of the circles in which we run are homogenous groups of singles, I think it's time to find some teenagers or grandparents we can link up with and do life with. While we're mixing and mingling with people from other walks of life (and other Sunday-morning classrooms), we can politely let them know there are indeed singles in our church, and happy, nonpouty ones at that!

The Single Life Needs Good Ambassadors in the Church

Another great experience I had in my current church was serving on our outreach committee for a few years. I was asked to join by the committee chair, Jeanette, who was also the wife of one of my coworkers (and whom I secretly suspect simply needed more warm bodies with which to fill the committee). I didn't care about the motivation for the invitation, or about the fact that the main objective of this group—reaching out to those who don't yet know Jesus—was far from my forte. I saw a potential community-building experience, a chance to grow, and an opportunity to get to know Jeanette, a woman who seemed to have a flair for fun. The relationship with this wife and mom of one was just the tip of the iceberg of the good things that happened when I joined this crew.

As we planned evangelism training courses and events to which people in the church could invite their friends who didn't know Jesus, I developed relationships with this fun group. I was a good decade younger than the rest of the committee members and the only single one, but they embraced me just the same. Almost more so, as I became a younger sister of sorts to the group. As we all warmed up to each other, they would teasingly, yet lovingly, inquire about my love life, and I gradually became brave enough to offer my singles perspective to the publicity pitches they were considering for various events.

Someone in the group had the inspired idea of calling our outing to a Shakespeare play at a local outdoor theater "Shakespeare in Shorts." I loved it—but the rest of the flier wording... not so much. I don't remember the specifics, but it was something about inviting other couple friends for a fun summer outing. During one of our planning meetings, I muttered, "You know, single people like Shakespeare, too." The living room in which we were sitting suddenly grew silent. *Uh-oh.*

"You know, I never thought about that," said one of the word-meisters. "Wording it this way would make singles feel left out, and we definitely don't want that." Over the next ten minutes we finalized a flier we *all* felt happy about. And as the weeks and months progressed, these new friends started asking me more and more for the singles perspective for plans and wording. They were amazingly receptive to my "speech" about the word "family" being exclusive rather than inclusive, since we singles don't really fit this description ("You mean I'm supposed to bring my out-of-state parents to the church picnic?!").

I realized I had the ear of our senior pastor, who was also a member of the committee. He listened intently as I shared how all-inclusive language could be easily reached with the insertion of a few "friends" and "roommates" on fliers and in sermons usually addressed to spouses and children. Suddenly I also realized I'd become a spokesperson for singles in our church. And that was due at least in part to the fact that I'd been willing to stray beyond the singles group and, in the process of serving the church at large, share my perspective as a single.

Home for the Holidays

*L*ast Thanksgiving I wasn't just the third wheel, I was the eleventh. I was at my parents' for the weekend, and the gathering consisted of my mom and dad, my sister and brother-in-law, my grandmother and granddad, my grandma and grandpa, my sister's mother-in-law and father-in-law—and me. So basically, couple, couple, couple, couple, couple, and Camerin.

My parents had put as many leaves in the table as they could find, bless them, so at least I wasn't stuck at some lone kids' table—where people in my family usually sit until they marry and "graduate" to the adults' table. (At the rate I'm going, I fear they may have to add the stipulation of going on Medicare as a means of graduation so I don't get stuck at the kids' table for all time!)

After stuffing ourselves with, well, stuffing and turkey, we played our usual game of Scattergories (the only board game my parents own) with the most logical teams—couples. Mom came to my rescue and retired to the kitchen to get a jump start on the dishes and graciously offered me my father as a partner. Considering we weren't nearly as in synch as the other 'til-death-do-us-part teams, we didn't do so bad.

After the game, we pried Mom from the kitchen and settled our overstuffed bodies onto every sitable surface in the living room. To allow my sister and her new husband to create a few traditions of their own, my mom had prearranged for them to have the floor at this point. They led us in a round of thanksgiving, a great way to get to know the new faces in our midst and to commemorate the main point of the day (besides the ever-popular food and football!).

My gregarious brother-in-law, Bob, started—and, as to be expected, was most thankful for his new bride. His introverted, blushing bride simply seconded his appreciation of their new union. In a move that nearly brought us all to tears, my usually quiet grandpa quoted a love poem and told us he was most thankful for my grandma, the woman with whom he'd shared more than five decades of living and who was slowly slipping away into the shadow of Alzheimer's.

Looking at this aging yet faithfully loving pair, the hand-holding newlyweds nearby, and the rest of the happy couples I'm blessed to call family seated around me, my plans to say I was most thankful for a recent vacation to Germany changed. Suddenly I wasn't the singled-out member of the family, I was the awestruck spectator—and beneficiary—of a room full of faithfulness and love.

And suddenly it was my turn.

Never one to think well on my feet (that's why I'm a writer!) and caught up in the swell of bittersweet emotions, I stammered out something about being most thankful for the examples of godly love and faithfulness seated around the room—then burst into tears. (I do this so easily, I think it may be one of my spiritual gifts!) My grandmother handed me a tissue (don't they always have these in hand?), my sister's pragmatic in-laws started squirming, and Mom once again saved the day by quickly taking her turn next.

Dabbing my eyes and composing myself, I listened to the rest of the group's thoughts and thanks. I was dreadfully embarrassed by my uncontrolled emotions until my dad mentioned that the combined total of the marital commitment in the room was somewhere upwards of 160 years. Then it hit me that these people were experts at for-better-or-for-worse and had big hearts, making them well-equipped to handle my little emotional outburst and all my other countless quirks.

Soon the thanksgivings were through, and we were all happily snarfing pumpkin and pecan pie. But as I sat in this sea of couples, chatting and laughing, I sent out one more thanks—this time without words or tears—directly to the One who gives all things worth being thankful for, that maybe I wasn't so alone after all.

There's No Place like Home

The jumble of emotions I felt on Thanksgiving captures the role our families play in our singleness. They can help make it satisfying and meaningful, or they can help make it awkward and miserable. And usually these feelings can all occur during the course of one family meal.

When you're single, family gatherings can be the best of times and the worst of times. In the course of one afternoon, we can eat more homemade food than we've seen in a month, field more loving, albeit sometimes nosy, questions about our welfare than we've answered in six months, and receive more hugs and kisses than we've been given in a year. When our family is fairly functional, these gatherings can be just the lovefest we need to get us through a dry spell or lonely season. And if our family is not-so-functional, it can make us appreciate our singleness, the solitude and harmony of our own home, and our decision to wait until we've found someone functional before getting hitched.

Then there are the family gatherings that make us want to run screaming from whoever's house we're meeting at for that particular holiday. These are the days when well-meaning but clueless Aunt Marge sits us at the kids' table, Grandma mentions for the 407th time that she really hopes she's still alive when we finally get married, and our adorable but tact-deprived nephew asks why we don't have a husband. My friend Cathy complained once that her married siblings always seem to find excuses for not helping in the kitchen during family meals. And these excuses usually involve having a spouse and/or kids—leaving her excuseless and stuck with KP duty.

Family gatherings can be stressful enough without throwing in sensitive issues of family and worth. And we women can read meaning into the slightest glance, seating arrangement, or offer of another helping of mashed potatoes. If we're seated at the end of the table, we feel singled out, like any minute a spotlight will flash on us and we'll be fired twenty questions about our latest efforts to find a mate. If we're seated between couples, we feel like the highlighted square in the Sesame Street "One of These Things Is Not Like the Others" game. (Why can't furniture manufacturers somehow devise a table that seats an odd number of people?) If we're asked to bring something edible, it has to be delicious enough to prove we don't eat so much fast food that we've forgotten how to cook, and yet not so gourmet that people will think we spend all our time at home cooking instead of getting out once in a while. If we bring a guy home, we know he'll be scrutinized mercilessly and sized up as a potential addition to the family's gene pool. If we don't bring anyone home for enough family gatherings in a row, we're harassed or told about the virtues of our uncle's paperboy, dentist, or cubicle mate.

My friend Kathryn recently told me about the challenge of convincing her family to let her host a family holiday gathering at her condo—even for a "lesser" holiday, such as Mother's Day. They didn't want this single woman (a group not necessarily known for their domestic skills) to go to all the effort to host a houseful of family all by herself, while she just wanted to do her fair share of the entertaining—and to give the moms in her family a break on their special day.

Since I live in a different state than all my family members—except for a married cousin who's younger than me—I can't bring a dish to our gatherings. And my mom seems to always shoo me out of the kitchen so I can catch up with the aunts, uncles, and grandparents I haven't seen since the last holiday. This means I usually end up keeping my granddad out of trouble (see chapter 8 for more on this).

Tradition!

Another challenge unique to single women is the expectation that we'll always be at family holiday gatherings. Our married siblings may tire of the tug-of-war between both sides of the family, but at least they have some options when it comes to the holidays. And when they have kids, they even get the option of staying home and creating their own traditions. Wow.

I thought this wasn't an option for me (proving an important point that sometimes these limitations are self-imposed rather than created by my family) until several years ago when a couple of my single friends suggested a Thanksgiving getaway. Four of us single girls were going to jet off to San Antonio to eat, shop, sightsee, and giggle our way through Thanksgiving weekend. But would our families go for it? Would they allow us to miss traditional family gatherings for such a frivolous trip?

Surprisingly, yes.

While a couple of these friends celebrated early with their families, we all went with the blessings of our parents and extended relatives. Some even asked us to check out this new vacation destination for them. And our time together was great, though anything but traditional. We ate peanuts on a plane instead of turkey on a platter on Thanksgiving Day (followed by even-less-traditional Mexican food for the next several days).

In between seeing the Alamo, trolleying to nearby missions and historic districts, shopping for Mexican blankets, and watching Independence Day on a giant IMAX theater screen, we had a great time laughing together and forging our own brand of holiday fun.

Last year I missed my family's Christmas gathering because I was visiting my friends in Germany. I had just enough vacation days left to eke out a decent trip, and my friends found me a dynamite airfare from a Germany-based travel agent. Once again, my family graciously let me go, guilt free. Some even gave me early Christmas checks earmarked for souvenirs or sauerkraut-covered meals. And my mother's words during one phone conversation before I took off meant the world to me. "We never want you to feel obligated to come home for the holidays," she said. "You are always, always wanted here, but we never want you to feel guilted into visiting. We know you need to create some traditions of your own and to take opportunities when they arise." With this blessing, I went with peace—and had a marvelous time. And my next visit home was that much sweeter, because it was a choice, because it had been paced with some other kinds of trips, and because I knew it wasn't taken for granted. By my parents—or me.

If you like to travel, and if holidays are one of the few times you can get away (as is the case with my teacher friends), why not go for it? Your family may be more understanding than you think. And if they aren't, buy them great souvenirs and maybe they'll rethink their stance. Seriously, though, they may not be wild about you missing a family holiday gathering, so choose your battles wisely and remember that you are an adult who's

Single Stuff

www.ChristianityToday. com/singles

Okay, I'll admit this is a shameless plug for the site I work for. But there really are great articles, message boards, chats, and personals—all from a Christian perspective. Check it out!

going to make choices that your family might not always understand or agree with. That doesn't mean you love or respect them any less. It just means you have your own life to live.

Maybe you want to start smaller and create a few holiday traditions of your own. I used to get a lot of free books at my job, so throughout the year I'd save one or two that I thought each family member would enjoy. Then I'd wrap them in the Sunday comics and present them (with the explanation that they were freebies from my office) on Christmas Eve (since we're a Christmas-morning gift-opening family). It was fun to add a little contribution of my own to my family's annual celebration. Just because you're single doesn't mean you shouldn't put some thought and unique spin on your holiday celebrations. Get creative. Get meaningful. And get a kick out of being a full-fledged contributing member of your family.

Family Ties

Some of your family members may never make peace with or truly understand your single life. And while that can be difficult and unfair, making peace with it yourself is still an absolute necessity. When they see you living a happy, fulfilling life, they'll eventually find some peace in your lack of panic and pathetic brooding. And while you can't change their expectations of you, you can change your expectations of them. Don't expect them to ever fully understand your singleness (and if they ever do, bonus!). Seek less to fulfill their dreams for your life and focus instead on making the most of God's unique path for you.

Recently I received an unexpected letter from my grandmother. I don't know what prompted it, but I know I will treasure its contents always. Especially the last line—"Always know that we love you, that with God's help we will try to provide the love and assurance that whoever you choose to be, whatever you choose to be—married or single, famous or just average Joe—you are what we always wanted, one of five granddaughters for whom I will always thank God—and don't you forget it." I think my happiness as a single is rubbing off on my family, and their unconditional acceptance is rubbing off on me. It's a wonderful dynamic that's been years in the making, for which I'm exceedingly thankful. And yes, Grandmother, I'll never forget.

Oh, Mother!

My friend Cathy confided in me recently that she feels her parents worry about her much more than they do about her married siblings. I can definitely relate. No matter how far women's lib has taken us, there's still an underlying feeling—at least among older generations—that women need to be taken care of. While there's part of me that chafes at the old-school vein of thought that says I need a man to be safe and secure in this big, bad world, I have to admit, there are times I wish I could relax into someone else's care. Mostly this is fatigue speaking and not some erroneous notion that I'm somehow weaker as a woman or a single. Let's face it, independence is tiring at times!

Cathy and I and countless other single women with worried moms and dads know that our parents mean well. It's just a God-given concern for our welfare that doesn't stop no matter how old, financially independent, tae-bo trained, or household-repair proficient we become. It makes me think of the verse in Genesis (2:24) that talks about children leaving their mother and father and cleaving to their spouse. There's nothing said about those of us who leave and have yet to find a cleave-er (I don't think my childhood crush on Wally Cleaver counts!). That makes for confusing roles and conflicting expectations. In my family, this is most prominent in my relationship with my mom.

Mama Mia

I think a high capacity for worry is a prerequisite for becoming a mom, and my own mother passed this test with flying colors. When my sister and I were little, Mom would worry when we crossed the street to go to the park. When I was in high school, my mom worried that I wouldn't get good enough grades to earn me a scholarship into a "good enough" college. When I decided to go into journalism, she fretted that I wouldn't be able to support myself. And though she tries to mask it, I can tell there are times, as the years go by, when she fears I'll never find the love of my life. I know this fear is rooted in love and concern and, somewhat, the fear of the unknown. You see, my mom was never really single. She married my father when they were both in college, meaning she pretty much went straight from her parents' home to her husband's. And she had both my sister and me by the time she was my age.

The latter dynamic is extremely common among single women my age. Since women are waiting longer and longer to get married, we're pioneering a whole new demographic—which is simultaneously exhilirating and scary. And, at times, intimidating for the older generation, who weren't given nearly as many options as we are and who weren't really equipped to prepare us for the unique challenges of singlehood. Mother-daughter relationships are challenging enough without a whole demographic shift thrown into the mix.

For example, I'm amazed that by my age, my mother had put herself through college (the first in her family to reach this level of education), married my father, been a teacher for a couple years, had two daughters, and quit working to become a stay-at-home mom. I marvel at all my mom accomplished by this tender age. I'm not sure I would have done as well as she did in all these feats.

And yet, there are ways in which I feel more independent than she was and even is today. I've landed a job, moved to a new state, purchased a car, found two different apartments, and traveled to seven different countries, all by myself. There are times my mother has openly marveled at my accomplishments, and then I get a feeling that's both liberating and weird all at the same time.

It's taken me some time and some conversations with other single girlfriends who have I-love-you/you-make-me-crazy relationships with their own mothers to figure out the many reasons why Mom is the one person who drives us crazy the most. My theory is that the loving concern our moms show us, though comfortingly familiar and reassuring, also makes us feel all of eight years old. And for single people who already feel like there's a societal assumption that they haven't quite joined the ranks of the grown-up world since they haven't settled down with a husband, kids, SUV, and nice house in the burbs, this can be especially frustrating. My former roommie, Karen, talks about the fact that people assume she's younger than her sister, Debbie, who's actually three years younger than Karen, because Debbie has a husband, son, condo, and Suburban.

Single Stuff

"I Am Not Alone"
by Natalie Grant

You know it's true that God is always with you, but sometimes you still *feel* all alone in this big, bad, everyone's-paired-off-but-me world. Natalie sings this simple truth with such conviction, you can't help but be inspired and sing along. And when you do, listen to yourself—and believe it.

Karen and the rest of us single women are in no hurry to feel like a kid again when around our moms. We're too busy reminding the rest of the world—and sometimes ourselves—that we are adults (no matter how zany we may act when we're home alone!). What's been comforting to me is hearing women who are married and even decades older than me talk about feeling eight again when at home with their parents. It's really helpful to learn that sometimes this is an across-the-board parent thing, not just a single thing.

My mom's protective concern for me used to drive me nuts (and still does, I must admit, on days when I start to lose perspective). Even though I'm now thirty, she wanted to come see my new apartment asap so she could make sure it was safe (and was visibly relieved when she learned I'm now two blocks from a police station). During one visit home, she wouldn't let me go meet my dad at his office for lunch because there was "too much ice on the streets." (Never mind that I've driven across the Midwest in winter storms.) I've always known these requests are only made out of love and concern for my welfare. And I've come to realize that my annoyance is only motivated by a childish desire to prove myself.

I Am Single, Hear Me Roar

There's this need I've come to recognize in my growing number of single years to show my family, coworkers, church cohorts, married friends, and pretty much the whole world that I don't *need* a man. I hate those pitying "you poor dear, still single after all these years" looks that people can knowingly and unknowingly give—and the erroneous assumption that we women need a man to get by—so there's part of me that tries to overcompensate by proving that I can do it all myself. (Which, of course, means I come across more like a stubborn two-year-old than a self-sufficient grown-up!) And with no one does this stubborn streak seem to be stronger than with my mom.

Some time in my midtwenties, after a number of verbal clashes over my attitude-filled attempts to assert my independence and my mom's seeming failure to comprehend that I was truly an adult, I finally broached the topic of our shifting relationship one day over the phone. I gingerly explained that even though I hadn't had that universally recognized "graduation" from childhood to adulthood—marriage—I still paid bills and taxes, dealt with coworkers and deadlines, and cooked and cleaned just like all the other grown-ups I knew. "Mom, you do realize I'm an adult now, don't you?" I uttered.

"Yes," she replied. "I'm so proud of who you've become. But you do know that you'll always be my baby, don't you?"

When I saw the situation in this context and realized that several of my married friends and coworkers also feel like a child again whenever they visit their parents, my attitude softened. And as the years go on and there's no one special guy calling me "baby," having parents who still count me as one of the most treasured human beings in their lives means more and more to me.

After that conversation, my mom began asking me more about my job and my hobby of furniture refinishing. And I began digging deeper into the rich resource of her fifty-plus years of living. Swallowing my pride, I asked her which brand of vacuum cleaner she thought was best, when to leave a volunteer ministry for another opportunity, and the mother-of-all-questions, how do I know if he's Mr. Right? As we began meeting each other in the middle, acting more like peers, a wonderful friendship emerged.

Months later I called my parents' house, in tears. My dad answered the phone. Hearing my sobs, he asked if I was okay and if he should get Mom. At my meager "uh-huh," he went off in search of Dr. Mom.

"Honey? What's wrong?" Before I could get a word out, I burst into tears. Just hearing the sound of her voice—the same voice that had read my favorite book, *Andrew Henry's Meadow,* to me 512 times when I was a child, had taught me how to make Snickerdoodles and Rice Krispies Treats, had scolded me when I broke a window by throwing rocks, had cheered me on during high school drill team performances, and had sung heartily next to me in church—melted me to tears. Such history. Such comfort. Such love. When I was finally able to speak, I told her about the breakup that had just taken place, knowing her love would help carry me through the crisis.

Since then, Mom's proven to be a great student of the unique dynamics of the single life, trying to offer helpful advice whenever she can and learning to accept the path God currently has me on. I'm learning to glean more from her married-woman perspective and chafe less at her expectations, as I accept their source more in the context of her experience and love and less in terms of my falling short. Communication has been vital to our strong relationship. Through the tears and laughter and educational conversations, we've developed a friendship—one I treasure about as highly as any I have. Having an open mind and understanding heart with your own mother can be a huge help.

Mama Never Said There'd Be Days like This

Our frustration can also stem from the fact that we didn't receive enough preparation for the single life. The occasional days when loneliness, longing, and fear of spinsterhood loom especially large are tough. And the fact that no one warned us there'd be days like this can make them even tougher.

Also, it's equally frustrating when Mom's view of what is "best" for us includes a husband and kids—the brand of happiness with which they, and most everyone else, are most familiar. Trying to convince ourselves that the single brand of happiness can be just as great as the married brand of happiness can be tiring enough without also trying to convince Mom, the person whom we want to please most. Letting ourselves down from the life we'd expected is one thing; letting our moms down is a whole different level of difficult. And it's no one's fault— not theirs for wanting the traditional model of "success" for us, not ours for not creating this kind of success in our life. But it's important to realize that both we and our mothers want the same thing: a fulfilling life for us. When the issue is differing expectations, communication is key.

So what's your relationship like with your mother? Is she loving? Demanding? Understanding? Disappointed? Wherever you're at with Mom, a good heart-to-heart conversation could go a long way in the promotion of mutual understanding, reassurance that you're happy just as you are (of course, you need to reach this point of contentment first!), and revised expectations for each other.

Leading Men

"How are you?" (slight pause for response). "How's your love life?" *This* is how my granddad greets me whenever I see him at family gatherings. Considering the fact that these are usually holidays—and the fact that I never seem to time my few dating relationships around these coveted times to be paired off—I typically have nothing to say. So my part in this little warped tradition goes something like this: "Great, Grandpa, thanks for asking." (Longer pause to try to come up with a response that's funny, or intelligent, or just not terribly pathetic.) "Um, well, not so existent right now, I guess you'd say." (Okay, I didn't say I ever *succeed* in any of these quests!)

To be honest, his persistent inquiries into this elusive part of my life—not my job, my friends, my church, even my health (something the older generation seems to love to talk about)— used to really irk me. Other areas of my life are usually going pretty well, moving forward even, as areas of life are supposed to. But, no, he chooses to fixate on the one area of my life that refuses to offer a tidy answer. So right off the bat, I'm tongue-tied and feeling like less of a person since the one area of my life he seems to take interest in yields nothing but awkward silence.

I've protested against the question, which usually leads me nowhere with this ornery old guy who loves to argue for argument's sake. And would I really want to "win" against my grandpa anyway? Besides, when I try that route, I get the sneaking suspicion people in the room are thinking, *No wonder she's single; she's so defensive and argumentative.* Sigh.

Single Stuff

Ever After

The best scene in this modern-day-flavored Cinderella story is when the prince finally realizes Drew Barrymore, a.k.a. "Cinderella," is the gal for him and rushes to save her from the evil villain who's kidnapped her. But when he arrives at the bad guy's castle, he isn't met by a damsel in distress but by a strong woman who's just saved her own hide and is walking out of the castle on her own two feet. You go, girl!

I've tried just going ahead and offering details about other areas of my life that are going well. But considering my grandpa is the man who dreamed his grandchildren would follow in his footsteps and go into the Coast Guard (mind you, we all grew up in Kansas) and doesn't believe in any job where you aren't your own boss (he started and has run his own plumbing business for years), this leads to all kinds of other conversations where I fall short of his expectations. Another sigh.

My best effort was when I followed up his question about my love life with a question about his. Flustered, he retorted, "You aren't supposed to ask about that," with a twinkle in his eye that said he either secretly respected my gutsy question or that my grandmother was a happier woman than I cared to know about. But, undaunted, I proceeded with a SingleGirlPower speech about how it isn't fair that single people's love lives are an open book. For some reason, it's perfectly appropriate for marrieds to ask us if we're seeing anyone, and if we are, then "How's it going?" and "How serious is it?" And if we aren't, then "Why not?" and "Have you thought again about my cousin Frank?" But somehow it raises all kinds of eyebrows if we turn the tables and ask something such as, "So how's your marriage? You two getting along okay? Has he kissed you lately? What's that like?"

But in the end, my solution with my granddad simply left us *both* offended. There was still an awkward pause, and I still felt the unspoken thought lingering in the room, *What an attitude. No wonder she's still single!*

We Only Harass the Ones We Love

Really, though, I love my granddad dearly. Even though I'm still traumatized by the time in junior high when we ate out at a pizza joint and he took home not just our leftovers, but the leftovers from the two tables next to us, there's something inherently charismatic and likable about this feisty old guy.

At no time was this more apparent than the year when he didn't make it to our family Christmas gathering. My grandmother wasn't feeling well, and he'd stayed home to help take care of her. I missed their presence around our dining room table but was relieved to be off the hook for another round of love-life questioning. Or at least I thought I was off the hook.

Shortly after my aunt arrived from the same town where my grandparents live, she pulled me aside. "Your grandfather gave me strict instructions to ask you about your love life," she said, smiling at this well-known family tradition. I sighed and was ready to launch into a verbal tirade about how nothing in my life was private and sacred, when she said something else that changed my tune. "He said you wouldn't know he loved you if he didn't ask about your love life."

Huh. So that's what he'd been trying to communicate all this time? Wondering why a simple "I love you" wouldn't suffice, I thought of my recent observations of men and their insatiable need to protect and provide for their families. As I'd been talking with male friends and coworkers, I'd noticed a whole different motivation for their efforts from nine to five. It wasn't just to find meaning in life or to earn a paycheck (as most working women I knew were motivated); it was also part of a larger need to provide for the people with whom God had entrusted them.

I'd also noticed a similar phenomenon in my parents, who displayed a greater concern for my welfare than they usually did for my married sister (who was entrusted to my brother-in-law's care). Though part of me bristled at this apparent need to be cared for, which seems to be unique to women and even more pronounced in single women, when I looked at this dynamic less through prideful eyes and more through the eyes of a loving daughter and granddaughter, I began to appreciate the care and concern. It sure beat the alternative! And in lieu of a husband to care for me, it was nice to know there were several family members looking out for my well-being.

When I looked at my grandfather's nagging questions about my love life in this context—and in the context of his generation, which married so much earlier and in which women had few if any options of their own—my heart softened. This was his way of making sure his family was okay. More specifically, that I was okay—three states away and all by myself in the big, bad Windy City. Though I still wished I could find the perfect witty comeback for his "how's your love life" inquiry, I simply told my aunt to pass on that there was nothing exciting to report in that area of my life. "Oh, one more thing," I added. "Tell him I love him, too."

Daddy's Girl

I was shocked several years ago when I started crying in the middle of a counseling appointment. The tears didn't surprise me as much as their source: my dad. Somehow he'd come up in conversation, and all at once there were tears. Through some carefully calculated conversation (for which I was paying more than I wanted to think about!), I figured out that somewhere within me was a desire for a deeper relationship with my dad. I thought back to our phone interactions whenever I called home. Dad would usually pick up, offer the latest Mr. Courtney joke (read: corny but cute) and some chitchat about the weather in both our geographic locations, and then say, "I'll get your mother," before disappearing somewhere in search of my mom. I could see how this type of interaction wouldn't lead to a deep relationship, but was this really bothering me enough that it was taking up negative space somewhere deep in my psyche?

Disturbed, I dared broach the topic with a couple close single girlfriends. I didn't reveal my issues but innocently asked about their relationships with their fathers. My friend Julie said her conversations with her father also revolved around the weather. My roommate, Karen, admitted that her phone calls home yielded the same one-liner from her pa: "Let me get your mother." Lisa said her father never asked, "How was your day?" or "How's your job?" but never failed to inquire, "Your car running okay?" Hmmm. I was beginning to notice a trend—a lack of depth with Dad.

As I began to think and talk about possible "whys" for this semidisturbing phenomenon, the best solution seemed to be generational. Our dads are of a generation that didn't express emotions, that hadn't been encouraged to get in touch with their softer side, that wasn't raised to ask about personal thoughts and experiences.

Though emotions are now safer territory for our male peers, this grace hasn't yet been extended to or accepted by generations that have come before. All the same, these men are still the main men in our life, so our expectations of them can run high. The result is a sad disparity between our needs and expectations and our father's emotional availability. No one's fault, really. Just an unfortunate result of changing family dynamics over the years.

Never one to keep this kind of thinking and wrestling to myself, I regurgitated all these thoughts and theories—as well as my surprising counseling experience—to my mom the next time we chatted on the phone, with strict instructions not to tell Dad. (I didn't want to hurt his feelings and wanted to bring it up myself if I ever deemed it helpful.) Mom listened and related somewhat with me in regard to her own relationship with her father. As I contemplated both my parents' fathers—especially my dad's quiet, seemingly emotionless father—I realized this emotional evolvement went back farther than I had thought. And, of course, my mother, never one to be able to keep anything from my dad, told him all about our conversation.

I was angry at her and concerned about my dad's feelings—until my next visit home, when *he* brought up the topic in a rare father-daughter lunch. In between awkward pauses and bites of pizza, we discussed my desire for a deeper relationship. He explained that he usually passed the phone off to my mom whenever I called home because he knew how much we loved chatting with each other. (Oh, these men and their perplexing expressions of love!) I told him how much I appreciated this sentiment, but that I called home to talk to him, too.

Our conversation that day was occasionally stiff but quite revelatory. We broadened our vocabulary with one another—talking about thoughts and feelings we'd never discussed before—as well as our understanding of each other. When our lunch was over, we were full of pizza and, more important, ideas of ways to deepen our relationship (starting with more father-daughter lunches).

Since that awkward lunch years ago, I've learned fascinating things about my dad's job and childhood (now that he knows I *want* to know these things). Though sometimes he still passes the phone off to my mother after a quick joke and comment on the weather, there are other times when just he and I talk—and he fills in my mom later on a need-to-know basis. We've enjoyed lunches and dinners together, just the two of us, sometimes chatting nonstop, other times enjoying the comfortable silences. And through it all I've gained a greater knowledge of my father and a stronger self-esteem, armed with our meaningful interactions and his words of love for me. Every time he calls me his "beautiful daughter" (which took some positive reinforcement to get him to realize how much I love this), I grow inches taller, my need for male attention and approval gets met in healthy ways, and my singleness becomes that much more doable.

What Are Friends For?

My fridge is plastered with pictures of four of my favorite friends—Karen, Julie, Ruth, and Lisa. There's a picture of us crammed on a bench on Chicago's Navy Pier, one of us in flannel pj's the morning after a New Year's Eve slumber party several years ago, and a shot of us decked out to go to a swanky German restaurant to celebrate Lisa's birthday. These photos bring back fond memories of good times shared with my little gang.

The mental snapshots I have of this family of sorts are perhaps even more treasured. There's the time Karen and I went trunk-diving for brownies that were erroneously stored out of reach during a road trip with Julie and Lisa. While everyone was laughing so hard they could barely breathe, I folded down my section of the back seat and started rooting through the trunk for the chocolate treat (don't try this at home!). When I finally found the coveted Tupperware container, a cheer went up from our funny foursome, and laughter filled our car for miles and miles of Wisconsin highway.

Another memory isn't quite so humorous but is equally treasured. Many years ago, when The Girls and I were gathering to celebrate Julie's birthday, I showed up in tears. My boyfriend of three years and I had just broken up that afternoon. I was miserable, but I wanted to honor my friend and knew I could use the company of these dear sisters. So I shared my sob story, cried some more, received a round of hugs, and then we all went out to eat to celebrate Julie's special day. Though my eyes were swollen and my heart was nearly broken, I felt safe and somehow hopeful surrounded by the love, laughter, and support of my family of friends.

I don't use the word "family" lightly here. The relationships I share with these dear Christian sisters go deep and represent a serious investment of time. And I don't mean to downplay or negate the role my biological family still plays in my life, or what role your biological family plays in your life. Nothing could ever replace the people who've known us since birth, seen us in diapers and any getup we sported during the seventies or eighties, shared with us everything from the joy of Christmas morning to the grief of family funerals, endured family vacations and sick days with us—and still love us anyway. Whether they were a positive influence in our life or a disastrous one, these people will forever be our family. But, as we discussed in the previous chapter, these roles change as we age. And if you're like me, these people live several states away. Though roles and geography may change, the need for a strong support network doesn't. Without a spouse or kids to fill our God-wired need for deep relationships, we need to look elsewhere. Enter friends.

Get Real

One key to the kind of deep, meaningful relationships we all need is being vulnerable. Social gatherings are great, but in times of lagging self-confidence, breakups, spiritual dry spells, and workplace woes, dinner and a movie doesn't always cut it. We all need the kind of friend we can call and cry to at 2:00 A.M. and who'll love us enough to confront us when we're going down a wrong road. But this kind of depth isn't reached without some vulnerability.

One of my newest friendships is with a woman at work whose brand-new marriage is in ruin. Before I discovered this awful truth, our conversations had centered around television, hairstyles, and the best place to find great, cheap shoes. But when she suddenly lost a lot of weight and often had puffy, tearful eyes, I finally pulled her aside one day and asked if everything was okay. She started explaining her suspicions that her husband of just under a year was having an affair, then let out a sob that makes me ache just remembering it. I gave her a long hug, we both cried, and over the next hour we exchanged the kind of gut-wrenching pain everyone experiences at some point in life but no one seems to want to talk about.

I was devastated to hear about her angry, deceptive husband, and she was surprised and somewhat relieved to learn that I, too, had suffered a bout of depression a few years back. As she contemplated the possibility of being single again after years of dating and marriage to the love of her life, we exchanged honest talk about the fears and freedoms of the single life. Since then, our conversations have been gritty, gut-wrenching, and, amazingly enough, marked by God's grace in rare moments of humor, in shared tears, in a deep level of connectedness that doesn't happen in everyday chitchat. Though I eagerly anticipate the day when this dear sister's pain isn't so oppressive, I treasure a friendship that's free of the pretension and prettying-up we Christians are sometimes guilty of.

Sex and the Single Girl

Another key ingredient for successful singleness that our friends offer is accountability. This can be tricky to establish and a bit awkward at times, but in this sexed-up society, it can also be a lifeline.

Look at this example from my life. During dinner at a trendy French restaurant years ago, my single girlfriends and I set a new record for ourselves: We waited a whole thirty minutes before we started asking "Camille" about the new man in her life, "Rick." They'd been dating for about four months, and we loved bringing up the only dating relationship happening among us—as a vicarious treat for those who were waaay between dating relationships, as a way of making sure Rick was Camille-worthy (one of the most important girlfriend duties!), and as a way to see Camille blush and gush about this great guy.

But this time, as we savored the French cuisine at our big round table, the conversation took a slightly different turn. Instead of blushing, Camille was squirming. Her answers to our questions about how things were going were vague. I began to fear Camille was experiencing doubts or that she and Rick secretly had broken up.

These fears were put to rest when she finally uttered what was eating at her: "We've been wrestling lately with where to draw lines in our relationship." There was a moment of silence as the rest of us processed what she'd said. I think we all knew from her tone and body language exactly what she meant—she and Rick were struggling with sexual temptation.

A couple of us who have experienced similar temptations in past dating relationships offered empathy and shared stories of our own struggles. Beth talked about napping with one of her previous beaus, a shared activity that seemed innocent enough to her but turned out to be a turn-on for him. That was the first—and last—time they "slept together." Jennifer talked about staying overnight with an out-of-town boyfriend. While the arrangements made sense logistically, and while they spent the night in separate rooms, the decision to stay together also led to some late-night goodnight kissing that went on and on and on.

I also shared about the guy I dated in college, my first real boyfriend (yes, I was a bit of a late-bloomer relationally!). He and I reveled in our first-time-away-from-home freedom by making out for hours at a time in his room. But we eventually admitted to ourselves that the time we spent alone kissing was killing our communication, leading to more temptation, and damaging our reputation as committed Christians on a secular campus. When I'd leave his room and arrive back in my own dorm late at night, I couldn't explain to everyone that we'd just been making out, not having sex, as many people assumed. Though it felt silly at the time, we finally set our own curfew—for the sake of our hormones as well as for the sake of the curious eyes around us.

As Camille shared her own temptations, she still seemed embarrassed and squirmy. Wanting to reassure her, I said, "If good Christian friends like us can't talk about this, what good are we? And if we don't talk about this, who are you going to dis-

Single Stuff

Coming to Life
by The Normals

Andrew Osenga, the single lead singer and songwriter for this Christian band, put some of the struggles of the single life to amazing acoustic pop/rock music. "Black Dress" voices the lure of temptation. "The Best I Can" speaks of making the most of where you're at, even if that's not what you'd envisioned or hoped for. "Coming to Life" talks about the futility of trying to find the love we truly long for in a romantic relationship. Deep stuff. Great for when you need to know someone sympathizes with those tough questions running through your head. Or when you need reminding of the Someone who's somehow the answer.

cuss it with?" More honest talk followed, and I sensed Camille relax enough to realize we didn't think less of her for struggling in this way. In fact, I greatly admired her honesty.

I suddenly remembered Ann, a good Christian friend who'd similarly opened up and shared with me years ago her sexual temptation struggles. Though then-naive me was shocked that she and her boyfriend (now husband) were wrestling in this way, I was also relieved that I wasn't alone in this struggle. For some reason, I'd grown up thinking "good Christian girls" don't have hormones and that drawing lines—which usually seems to be the female's responsibility in a relationship—would be an easy thing to do. When I found myself tempted and not so clearheaded in the heat of the moment, I remember feeling surprised, guilty, and fearful that I was an awful Christian. Hearing Ann's admission that day helped me realize I was simply a human being (complete with God-given hormones) who needed to have a serious heart-to-heart with God and my boyfriend about boundaries.

I also needed an accountability partner, I realized one was staring me right in the face. So Ann and I met regularly after that for lunches and coffee, asking each other difficult questions and wrestling with the age-old issue of "how far is too far?" While we didn't necessarily find any concrete answers, what we did find was just as valuable—the guts to bring to light our desires to go farther than we knew was good for us, our missteps along the way, and our uncertainty about where to draw lines. And, most important, we did so in the right context—with God and trusted Christian friends.

So that day in the French restaurant, I ended our talk by telling Camille how much I admired her vulnerability. Looking back, I hope I communicated to her, and the three other dear Christian friends seated with us, that it is okay to be that open when among friends. It's not easy for us singles to stay pure in this sex-saturated society, especially since the "just say no" messages directed at us from the church seem to taper off soon after high school. If we're too embarrassed to discuss sex in Christian circles, then I'd venture a guess that we aren't hearing enough of God's perspective on this much-misunderstood topic. And he's the One who created sex!

It's so easy for fear, pride, and guilt to keep us from sharing the messier parts of our life with each other, unfortunately robbing us of accountability and the kind of gut-level friendship God created for us within the body of Christ. It may be risky and embarrassing to be honest about our temptations and mistakes. But when it comes to sexual temptation, I've learned the stakes are too high not to.

Risks and Rewards

Over the past several years, I've shared with several close friends that I started going to a Christian counselor years ago to help me figure out a close-but-not-quite-right dating relationship. Two of these friends have since started going to counselors as well, to help them deal with the unique issues we all wrestle with in this fallen world. Being vulnerable has taught me that everyone—even the person who seems to have it the most "together"—struggles with some sort of pain. And it's taught me not to save this kind of life-sharing solely for a mate. There's so much richness to be experienced in relationships right now if we'll determine to live honestly and love freely.

I'll admit, there's more risk involved in going deep with people who haven't pledged to be with us 'til death do us part. These dear friends may move away, taking a piece of our heart with them. Schedules may change, workplace friendships may shift with changing roles, single friends may get married and become less and less available as they invest in their relationship with their new hubby (as well they should). Though there are no guarantees in any relationship (divorce and death are still unfortunate realities for married women, as is having children grow up and leave home), there are even less for single women who create a family out of their friends. But would a life without people who can make you giggle with just one sideways glance, who'll drive you to the airport at 4:00 in the morning, and who'll hold you when you've just suffered another breakup really be worth living?

10

We Are Family

*A*fter reading the last chapter, you may be saying, "Great! But where do I sign up? How do I get myself one of those family of friends?" Well, as you may have guessed, this isn't necessarily a quick and easy process. With your biological family, you were born and, ba-bing, instant family. A family of friends takes a bit more time and effort. But the good news is that you get to choose these people . . . unlike the annoying little brother you may have wanted to trade in for a pet dog or, on a more serious note, the verbally abusive mother you may have dreamed of running away from day after day as you were growing up. Now you're faced with a blank slate, a fresh start.

The Many Faces of Friendship

It's important to keep in mind that this "family" can take a variety of forms. Your close friends may all know and love one another, like my circle of friends does. Your group may include guys, à la the gang on *Friends.* You may opt for several deep and meaningful one-on-one friendships. Or you could go for the Bridget Jones model, where most of her interactions with her friendship foursome take place via phone. Some of this structure will be determined by your personality, geography, and schedule— and some will just evolve with the ebb and flow of your ever-changing life. Creativity and flexibility are key. So are . . .

Patience and Prayer

I distinctly remember driving down a street in Des Moines before my big move to the Windy City and mentally preparing myself for the lonely days ahead. *It's gonna be hard. Brace yourself,* I thought. Before I could degenerate into a full-fledged pity party, another thought hit me: *It doesn't have to be so tough.* It's as if God tapped me on the shoulder and reminded me oh-so-gently that he controls the universe, including my relationships. I was humbled and encouraged by his loving reminder, so I poured out my heart: *God, please provide some kindred spirits.*

His provision first came in the form of Christa and Jan, two wonderful single women I met at my office. As we interacted at meetings and staff coffee breaks, we discovered common interests in antiques, quirky romance movies, Edy's Grand Light French Silk ice cream, and earth-tone clothing. Our friendship soon blossomed. God had heard—and answered—my prayers. Lesson learned.

And it was a lesson I needed. Within a year of each other, Jan moved out of state for a ministry opportunity, and Christa married and moved overseas. When I felt back at square one with loneliness as a constant companion, I clung to the fact that the God who'd provided these dear friends in the first place hadn't changed. He would provide again according to his plan and time.

Get a Little Risky

The first time my former roommate, Karen, and I invited her coworker Lisa and my friend-of-a-friend Julie to join us for dinner one night many years ago, we had no idea what to expect. Lisa and Julie had never met—and Karen and I hadn't met each other's friend yet, either. Not exactly the ingredients for a sure-fire great evening! While we could've sat in awkward silence all evening, munching our chips and salsa, we were pleasantly surprised by the smooth flow of conversation and laughter.

You don't know the family potential of a group of friends until you try. Sure, it's risky. Sure, it may bomb. But the possibility of a circle of close-knit friends is well worth the risk of a lousy lunch or awkward shopping excursion.

The More the Merrier

My Fab Five actually started as a Fab Four. Julie, Karen, Lisa, and I used to frequent local restaurants and share many a Blockbuster night together. We've even gone on a few vacations together. What fun memories!

Then along came Ruth. She started out as "Julie's friend"; they'd met at church when Julie's family "adopted" Ruth, whose nearest relatives live hundreds of miles away in Puerto Rico. Julie invited Ruth to some of our get-togethers, and at first Ruth was very quiet. But as we learned to decipher her Spanish accent and appreciate her tell-it-like-it-is spunk, we discovered a friend who added new flourishes to our crew. Now Ruth is *our* friend, and we couldn't picture our family of friends without her.

Four Friends Every Single Woman Must Have

Whether you make these people part of your immediate family or extended family, having them in your life will lead to a more balanced and satisfying singlehood.

Married Friend

A couple years ago I had lunch with Carla and Annette, two Christian coworkers of mine who each have a marriage I admire. As we were talking about the upcoming wedding of a mutual friend, the conversation drifted to the topic of sex. While I blushed in silence, these frank friends told me that sex isn't always thrilling. Sometimes it's awkward and messy, they admitted. These friends aren't bashing their husbands; they're simply telling it like it is. And as a single woman in our sex-saturated society, I sometimes need to hear this. Through listening to my married friends over the years, I've learned better than to think that marriage is always chocolate and romance— or that it's a cure-all. Singleness may have its bad days, but married friends help remind us that life on the other side of the altar has its share of tough times, too. Additionally, just when we think a happy marriage is an impossibility, they give us a living example to the contrary. So find a friend whose marriage you admire, and watch and listen and learn.

Guy Friend

I met my friend Max years ago through a work connection, and nearly our entire relationship has transpired over the phone. Though we both live in the Chicagoland area, we're still nearly an hour drive from one another, so we don't get together very often (this whole phenomenon has caused The Girls to refer to him as my "little imaginary friend"). We've talked each other through job changes, breakups, parental woes, and milestone birthdays, and through it all I've gained priceless insight into the mysteries of the male mind. One of these insights is that it's foolish to expect men to play the role of a girlfriend in our life. But Max has helped fill the male vacuum in my life, helping me realize guy presence doesn't have to be an all (husband) or nothing (no husband) phenomenon.

Sympathizer

When my coworker Ginger announced her engagement, making hers the fourth wedding in our department in a year's time, I erroneously called my friend Max, seeking sympathy. After listening to him attempt to balance my perspective by rattling off a laundry list of things I have to be thankful for, I quickly and politely thanked him . . . then hung up and called the person I should have rung in the first place: Kathryn. With a mere five words I was feeling better already.

Me: "Ginger's engaged."

Kathryn: "I'm so sorry."

This single sister knew, without me having to explain, that I was so happy for Ginger's good news but also tired of being on the planning end of wedding showers. We both knew my jealous feelings were petty but fleeting. We both knew all the pros of the single life, were trying to make the most of this life stage, but also knew the inevitable reality of "singleness stinks days." And, most important, we realized these days get diffused with a little sympathy . . . and that they eventually give way to "singleness rocks days." Until the latter rolls around, sympathetic friends make life a little more bearable.

Cheerleader

Everyone needs to be celebrated in this big, bad world. And since we single girls don't have someone who's signed up to do this for life, we need friends who'll remind us we rock—right now, right where we're at. My friend and former roommate, Karen, has been this treasured friend in my life for the past decade. She's the queen of encouraging (and hilarious!) cards—

for holidays, birthdays, and no-reason-at-all days. She bought the birthday cake and Sesame Street "Happy Birthday" banner for my twenty-fifth birthday bowling bash (how else does one celebrate a quarter-century of living?!). One of the best antidotes to the erroneous there-must-be-something-wrong-with-me-because-I'm-single blues is a friend who'll celebrate God's blessings—big and small—with you.

Two Friends to Keep a Safe Distance From

Oh-Woe-Is-Me Wendy

All of us single girls have singleness stinks days. That's just an inevitable fact of life. But, unfortunately, so is the single woman who experiences these downer days 365 days a year. I'm not saying avoid her like the plague. On the contrary, she needs your encouragement, sense of humor, and singleness rocks days more than anyone. I'm just saying it might not be the best idea to make her your closest friend. Have fun with her, encourage her, pray for her, then make sure you get a fair amount of time away from her lest she sucks you into her black hole of despairing singlehood.

Nosy Nora

She may be your aunt, coworker, fellow church committee member, neighbor, or mother, but she's there—the woman who constantly asks about your dating life and always has a "nice young man" to set you up with (usually someone she just met in the produce department at the grocery store and about whom she knows nothing except he's single and breathing!). Again, enjoy your friendship—but also have a few clever but to-the-point comebacks planned, as well as time away from her. She'll make you paranoid or crazy (or some neurotic combination of the two) if you don't draw some definite lines.

Duking It Out with the Green-Eyed Monster

There's nothing more bittersweet to hear from a friend than, "I'm getting married." Well, if she's marrying a schmuck, it's just bitter, but if she's found a great man to do life with, we're so happy for her and yet so sad for the changes that will take place in our friendship. We know allegiances will shift from us to the husband—in fact, they've been shifting already during their dating season. We know Girls' Night Out will become trickier and less frequent. We know one of our common sources of commiseration and celebration—singleness—will slowly fade, and that she'll eventually forget what it's like to be single. And we know that when kids enter the scene, lunches out will come with new little giggly and wiggly companions and phone conversations will be sprinkled with side comments—such as, "Don't put that in your mouth!"—to her little darlings.

These are all inevitable, necessary, and healthy changes for her and a hands-on lesson in patience and selflessness for us. One of the main side effects of singleness is selfishness, since we typically don't have anyone else's needs to attend to on a daily basis. Having a friend get married and become a mom is a great model and antidote for this self-centeredness.

But what's challenging and unfortunate is that it seems we're always forced to be the understanding party, the one left behind. While our friend gets a new lifetime companion, we're left with a gaping hole. We're the one who graciously lessens the grasp on the friendship so the friend can become one with her new hubby or kids. And we're the one who plans a shower, wears a not-so-flattering dress in front of a churchful of people, and listens to every detail from the flowers to the frock, all the while smiling even though we desperately wish it was our turn.

My friend Ginger lost a roommate when her dear friend Amy got engaged. While she was thrilled for Amy, Ginger suddenly had to find a new home and some new stuff with which to fill it. It was definitely a bittersweet time of helping her friend plan a much-anticipated future, while prepping for her own uncertain, unchosen, and now more financially challenged one.

Similarly, after I'd been in Chicago for only one year, my dearest new friend in the area, Christa, got engaged. She and I had been like sisters from day one, and though her relationship with her boyfriend, Mark, was obviously a serious one, it hadn't affected our friendship much, since this military man lived halfway across the country. I'd loved chatting with Christa in that year about her faraway love, hearing about his latest military assignments, and sighing over portions of his love letters to her. In fact, I felt like I knew this guy, though I'd only met him once when he was in town for a short visit. Which is why it was especially painful when he didn't recognize me at the wedding. Sure, I knew he had much more important things on his mind that

Single Stuff

"True Companion"
by Marc Cohn

What's cool about this love song is that it not only talks about the rush of romantic emotions felt on a wedding day, but the beautiful desire to grow old together as a couple. Listen to the lyrics for a great portrait of long-term love.

day, but there was part of me that wanted to whine, "I know a zillion details about you and your relationship with Christa. You're ripping one of my dearest friends away from me, and you don't even recognize me?!" She was off on a new life of love and adventure too many states away, and I was left back at square one in this relatively new geographic location. Oh, woe is me!

However, as time went on and I found new friends, and as Christa settled into married life, I started visiting her on occasion. First in North Carolina, a part of the country I'd never seen before, and then in Germany, where Christa's husband, Mark, got stationed a year and a half into their marriage. Visiting them in Germany (all three times so far) has been a blast! I get free lodging, knowledgeable tour guides, and all the conveniences of a nearby American military base. I've been able to explore and fall in love with Europe solely because these friends live there. And with each visit, I've gotten to know Mark more and more (this time in person, instead of through Christa's lovestruck descriptions and stories). Over early-morning coffee chats and European excursions, I've found Mark to be funny, ornery, well-read, a neat Christian guy, a loving husband, a great dad—and now *my* friend. When all is said and done, I didn't really lose a friend, I gained one.

Probably the most important step in your quest for friends is simply to start. Sure, it's risky opening up to new people. And, yes, these friends may not show up overnight. But surely there's someone in your life right now—the coworker in the next cubicle, the guy next door in your apartment complex, the woman you've been exchanging friendly smiles with in your aerobics class—whom you can target with a simple conversation and invite to coffee. Some day years down the road you may look back on that interaction as the start of a beautiful friendship—as well as the beginning of a family of friends.

Maternal Urges
and Lusty Longings

This past Mother's Day, I was lounging poolside in San Antonio with three of my single girlfriends. My friend Julie had discovered a great airfare to this warmer destination, a perfect springtime escape from the erratic one-day-it's-spring, the-next-day-it's-winter weather in Chicago. Actually, I was a last-minute fill-in when one of the original four—the only married one in the bunch—had to stay home because one of her kids got sick. In all my glorious single-girl freedom, I was able to go with only one week's notice. I figured I could call my mom to wish her a happy Mother's Day just as easily from San Antonio as from Chicago.

Lounging there next to the pool in our hotel's amazing court-yard, my friends and I alternately slept, sunned, dipped in the pool, and read. We were the picture of luxury. I remember thinking, *It doesn't get any better than this.*

And then I saw a mother and her cute little pink-dress-clad daughter wander out to the pool area from the next-door dining room, where there was a lovely Mother's Day brunch going on. The girl pointed to the pool with toddler fascination, then turned back to her smiling mom. After a moment, the two silently joined hands and ventured back to their brunch—the picture of mother-daughter bliss.

In that moment, I felt a twinge of the feeling that I was missing out on something really important. That worry—that becoming a mother won't ever be an option for me—launches surprise attacks when I'm innocently admiring the magical smiles exchanged between moms and their children. Will I ever get the chance to experience those kinds of magical moments? What if "someday" never comes? What if my husband shows up after all my eggs are kaput? What if there isn't a husband in God's will for me? The women on that San Antonio trip were all single and older than me—and all would make super moms. I wonder if "someday" will ever come for them either. The chance that it might not seems so unfair.

And yet, who's to say what's truly fair? Is it fair that Sue, the mom whose place I took on the Mother's Day excursion, had to stay home with her sick kid? Is it fair that my mom only now, in her empty-nest years, is able to enjoy the freedom to jet off on spur-of-the-moment vacations? (Though I'm still convincing her of the need to do this!) Is it fair that unwed teenagers get pregnant at an alarming rate, yet several of my married friends and family members wrestle with infertility? Is it fair that my friend Marty just buried her twenty-five-year-old son, that her mothering years are cut off so prematurely? When you put our single questions in the context of all the fairness questions floating through people's heads and hearts, suddenly our situations don't seem so unbalanced. No one gets a guarantee. Magical moments aren't a given, but a tangible reminder of God's grace.

As I watched the mother and daughter walk away that Mother's Day morning, I looked again at my traveling companions. Ruth was making her way to the hot tub. Julie was turning another page in the novel she was reading. And Cathy was turning over on her lounge chair to even out her sun exposure. All the picture of single-girl bliss.

Right then the tough questions about the future and fairness could wait. I was too busy making the most of the place God had me—single and in San Antonio with The Girls. If motherhood is in my future, I'll make the most of that, too. One thing I do know is that God would have me run well whatever race he puts before me. The rest I have to leave up to him and trust in his greater plan and timetable.

Sleeping Single in a Lumpy Bed

The other night when I was sleeping, I kept being awakened by the fitted sheet on my bed. Apparently the elastic was shot on the corner closest to my head because it kept coming untucked and entangling me and my pillow. The thought of not only getting out of bed but of expending enough energy to strip the sheets off and put new ones on, seemed near torture to my groggy mind. So I spent the night alternately being entangled by my fitted sheet and retucking it in.

Newsflash to self: You need new sheets!

The problem is, I don't just need new sheets. I need a new bed. True confession: I still sleep in the same twin-size bed that's been my slumbering sanctuary since grade school, the bed that sported the Holly Hobbie sheets I adored when I was eight. I remember other fitful nights of sleep in this bed, trying to get comfortable and not to knock myself out with the cast on my broken arm—in the fourth grade! This bed has been with me through stuffed animals, childhood nightmares, homework, and tearful teenage traumas.

While it seems as though it should be in my parents' attic with the other relics from my childhood, it isn't. Instead, it and my down comforter are my only snuggle-companions on the long, cold nights of Chicago winters. And some days it's a stark reminder of my singleness. It makes me think of the title of one of Luci Swindoll's books: *Wide My World, Narrow My Bed.*

Practically speaking, the bed fits me just fine. I'm short and don't take up much room. I don't toss and turn much. And as a Christian single person, I sleep alone. Every night. For all of my three decades of living. Sometimes I look at the smallness of my bed and wonder if it's symbolic of the fact that I will continue to sleep alone for all the decades to come. I mean, even if I wanted to give in to the whims of this sexed-up society, logistically I'd have a few problems. Just what I need, one more thing to add to my potential-husband wish list. Wanted: Knight in shining armor—with king-sized bed!

I know God's command to save sex for marriage (Heb. 13:4; Gal. 5:19; Col. 3:5) is for our own good—physically, spiritually, and emotionally. I've heard too many stories of sexual regret to think my decision to honor this command is a bad one. And I've been told by many people that sex isn't always all it's hyped to be. But there are moments when neurotic thoughts fly through my head: *Will my husband get to see me naked before gravity and wrinkles get the better of my bod? Will I get to have sex legally (i.e. in the context of marriage) before I hit my sexual peak? What do I do with the hormones God gave me that occasionally get stirred by romantic movies, the* People *magazine hot bachelors issue, long goodnight kisses, or even a man's hand in the small of my back?*

Let's put it this way: If you'd told me when I was thirteen that I'd still have zits when I was thirty, I would've run screaming through the halls of my junior high. And if you'd told me in my early twenties, when I was fighting sexual temptation with my boyfriend, that I'd still be sexless at this age, I would have freaked out. It makes me think of that scene from *Disney's The Kid,* where Bruce Willis's character meets himself as a child, and mini-Bruce says something like, "Let me get this straight. When I grow up I have no wife, no dog, and I'm not a pilot?" With equal parts incredulity and horror, he yells, "I grow up to be a loser!" I'll admit, in this paired-off society and family-oriented church world, there are moments when I'm tempted to offer a hearty "amen" to that declaration—only in my own words. "You mean I'm thirty, I've got no husband, no kids, and no house in the suburbs? You mean I'm still sleeping in a single bed? I've grown up to be a loser!"

Symbolism aside, I really do need a new bed—now. All those years have taken their toll on my poor little mattress. I've turned and flipped it just about every way it can go and am running out of angles without sags and wayward springs. Recently, while waiting with friends to get seated at a restaurant, I popped into a nearby furniture store. I wandered over to the bed section to do some preliminary checking on prices—and nearly fainted onto one of those beds when I spied the tag. How can something you use primarily while asleep cost so much money? With my single income, being able to afford one of these bedtime beauties is about as likely as me finding that knight in shining armor.

Questions began to run through my head: *Should I try to save up just enough to buy another single bed, since there's no foreseeable need for anything more in the near future? Will I ever graduate to a "grown-up" bed? Can I eke out a few more years with my tried-and-true bed? And if all I get to do in bed right now is sleep, can't I at least have a decent place to do so?* Somehow these aren't the questions I thought I'd be asking at this point in my life.

I didn't think I'd be buying a bed alone at this age. I'm supposed to go bed shopping with my fiancé or husband, looking at all the options and considering how different models would

Single Stuff

Dating Big Bird
by Laura Zigman

Single woman Ellen Franck is torn between her love for her adorable niece (a.k.a."The Pickle"), her baggage-toting boyfriend, the demands of her divalike boss, and her own biological "gumball machine." A great read for single women with strong maternal urges.

look in our home—together. We're supposed to sit on the edge of one and lie back for a second, imagining lazy Saturday mornings together in this bed. Instead, it's single ol' me, not knowing what to buy, not being able to afford anything, and even being slightly embarrassed to buy sheets for my single bed. Wide my bed, narrow my choices.

But, thankfully . . . big my God. When I start to whine to him, I'm reminded we were never promised fairness (at least our understanding of it), fortunes, Sealy Posturepedic beds, or spouses. We're simply promised God's faithfulness. These are the times when my trust in Bible verses such as "My God will meet all your needs according to his glorious riches in Christ Jesus," (Phil. 4:19), and my hope in a God who over the years has provided me with two couches—one for twenty-five dollars and one for free—are tested.

Then I think back to all the praying and Bible reading I've done in the past three decades and realize most of it has been in my little bed. Somehow when I see my bed more as my own personal altar and less as a blinking "single and celibate" neon sign, I'm less anxious to replace it. Perhaps God still has a few lessons to teach me before he provides a new place for me to practice these spiritual disciplines. Perhaps I'm supposed to lean more on my constant Companion and Provider before he responds to this need. I don't know. But I'm starting to suspect that the answers won't be found in a furniture store, in winning the lottery, or in marrying a man with a well-furnished bedroom, but rather on my knees in prayer—right next to my narrow bed.

Missing Persons

Another surprise lesson from my unmet expectations has been the connection with others dealing with disappointment—such as my sister. She and I have developed a strange new bond lately. It's one I'd trade in a heartbeat, yet one I treasure nonetheless. It's a bond of loneliness and longing—she for a baby, me for a husband.

The parallels are plentiful and painful. We're both missing someone we haven't met yet, someone we can't seem to make appear with our best human efforts, someone everyone else has seemed to find so easily.

We've both had near misses. Me, a long-term dating relationship with a wonderful man who turned out to be not quite God's best for me. She, a baby she carried in her body and in her heart, yet never in her arms. While I don't even dream of comparing the pain of my breakup with the pain of her miscarriage, there's an odd kinship blooming from our losses and longings.

I was touched when my sister called recently to offer comfort when she heard that the only other single person on my staff just got engaged, making for the fifth wedding in our department this year. Married at thirty after a decade of near misses and dry spells, she understood my longing to join the "marriage club" and find my lifelong love. And I wept with her for the child she lost just weeks into her first pregnancy—her son or daughter, my niece or nephew. She's my only sibling, the only one who can make me an aunt. I long with her for the child who is yet to come into our family.

What makes the new bond with my sister even more bittersweet is her reserved nature. She's the classic responsible, introverted firstborn child, while I'm the extroverted, overly emotional baby of the family. Over the years, she's been the sense to my sensibility. In moments when I've longed to know her more deeply and to receive more than one-word answers to questions about her love life and work world, I never would have wished for it to happen like this.

Yet suddenly here we are, talking about her uterus and the single bed in which I'm still sleeping. In our phone conversations, I hear echoes of distant conversations between those little girls we used to be—playing house together and dreaming of the real-life husbands and kids we assumed we'd have by now. Life hasn't quite turned out the way we thought it would back then. And while we both have much to be thankful for— great jobs, loving family, strong faith—there are moments when our longings and emotions are so raw, when I experience another breakup or she mourns another negative pregnancy test, that they can't help but spill out in our heartfelt conversations. God's fingerprints are all over our deeper friendship, giving comfort and kinship when we've needed it most.

These are the moments when I marvel at our God who creates beauty out of ashes. Isn't it just like him to take the source of some of our greatest pain and turn it into something wonderful? Perhaps in allowing our future beloveds to be "late," God's teaching us to better love the ones already in our life. Perhaps he's strengthening our family bonds before he adds new members. Who knows? Not me. I've learned better than to try to outguess God. As surprised as I am that my sister's not yet a mom and I'm not yet married, I'm equally as surprised by the blessing he's birthed in the midst of these disappointments.

When and if our respective missing persons arrive, I'll be tempted to pull them aside and thank them for being a little tardy, because it gave me a chance to get to know and bond with my sister in ways I wouldn't have otherwise. And it's helped me trust God and his higher ways more.

This Isn't
What I'd Expected

I was reading *Bridget Jones's Diary* at my new lunchtime coffee-shop hangout when Madison, a cute little girl who's the daughter of one of the shop's managers, and her princess umbrella twirled into my midday Me Time. I—and Bridget—would have to wait as this six-going-on-twenty-one-year-old deemed me a captive audience of one (I got the impression that's all it took for chatty Madison to launch into her thoughts and observations about life).

So while her three-year-old brother played with plastic dinosaurs on the floor, her mom did important coffee-shop work behind the counter, and I nodded and occasionally sipped my megasized (read: small bowl) chocolate hazelnut latte (read: yum!), Madison told me all about her teacher, Mrs. Marshall, her classmates Melissa and Britney, her favorite shade of nail polish (a sort of bubble-gum pink she was currently sporting), and the daddy-daughter dance she would be attending that night. I smiled at her precociousness and wide-eyed wonder as she talked and twirled her pink umbrella decorated with pictures of Disney princesses Cinderella, Belle, and Ariel.

www. Single Stuff

www.solodining.com

This site's dubbed "the web site devoted to taking the bite out of eating alone." You'll find tips on how to be more comfy as a solo diner, lists of restaurants that cater to those eating alone, and other bits of info to increase your solo dining savvy.

In a surprise change of topic, Madison suddenly asked, "So, do you have any kids?" I hated to disappoint this sweet young thing, who was either looking for possible playmates (or another captive audience to chat with) or was just making polite conversation. "Um, no," I replied.

"Do you have a husband?" she asked next. *Oh, brother.* I resisted the urge to search for an "ask me about my marital status" sign on my body, which must be the reason everyone seems to ask me this. "Um, no."

With all the tact of a six-year-old, she blurted out, "You mean it's just YOU?!" Slight bewildered pause. "I have a mommy and daddy, a doggy, and a brother. And it's just YOU?"

Though I loved the fact that her dog came before her brother in her list of beloveds in her life, I was still annoyed. Here I was, explaining my singleness again—and this time to a six-year-old stranger!

As I pondered what to say, I looked again at this impressionable innocent and noticed that the princess trio also graced the back of her denim jacket. I realized that role models such as these also led me, when I was Madison's age, to believe that people came in sets of two. And as I grew up, they fed my disappointment when Prince Charming didn't magically appear on his white steed to sweep me off to his castle.

Part of me wanted to warn Madison that Prince Charmings are few and far between—and sometimes overrated. That realistically she is more likely to meet a few Beasts in her day than any princes in disguise waiting to be saved by her love. That the typical fairy-tale ending doesn't always happen, but that doesn't mean her only other option is to become Ursula, the dastardly diva of the deep blue sea.

I wanted to tell her about the joy of creating your own "castle," fighting your own battles, and living the kind of "happily ever after" that isn't limited to two people riding off into the sunset together but that looks a lot more like the "abundant life" promised us in John 10:10.

Instead, I spared her the lecture and decided to be a new brand of role model. "Yeah, it is just me," I replied without a trace of apology or defensiveness in my voice. "And I think that's okay, don't you?"

Madison thought about that for a moment, then replied, "Yeah, I do." Another sweet smile, another twirl of the Three Princesses umbrella. Eat your heart out, Cinderella!

God's Expectations

Recently in a service at my church, we sang a song based on Micah 6:8—"He has shown you, O man, what is good and what the Lord requires of thee. But to do justly, and to love mercy, and to walk humbly with thy God." Though our checklist of expectations for any given age may be long and detailed, I love that God's list is short and simple: Do justly, love mercy, and walk humbly with God.

That latter part, walking humbly with God, sounds an awful lot like not taking ourselves—and our expectations of ourselves—too seriously. That's a sentiment I've heard echoed in the words of several older women recently. Each has said that turning fifty or sixty was the most freeing thing for them; suddenly they didn't care anymore what others said or even thought of them. They've all loved the freedom of taking themselves less seriously and walking humbly in God's lavish love and unique path for them. And they've all told "young" me that the best is yet to come.

Taking a cue from Micah 6:8 and these older, wiser women, I started my thirtieth birthday hanging out at one of my local coffee shops—with God and a new novel (thankfully, another accomplishment of my twenties was learning to enjoy my own company). Then The Girls and I went to one of our favorite restaurants for an evening of yummy food, nonstop chatter, and loving laughter. It was a great celebration of all God's accomplished in and through me (and often despite me!) and of the simple joys of doing justly, loving mercy, and walking humbly with God. Armed with these goals for the coming decade, I think the best is yet to come.

You've Got Two Choices

So life hasn't turned out the way we thought it would. This we know full well. But what's more difficult to distinguish is what to do with this reality. The way I see it, we have two options.

Getting Stuck

When life doesn't look like we think it should, it's easy to live in a kind of holding pattern until the life we'd hoped for finally unfolds. We've all met people beyond their early twenties who are still stuck in "college mode," a sort of temporary existence marked by faux-wood furniture and a failure to adopt any sort of ambition or plan that doesn't involve landing a man. What's sad is that often we can get stuck in this mode without even realizing it. I know there have been times when I have. It's easy to kind of coast through life, subconsciously waiting for a husband to come along, thinking the marriage will not only launch our life together, but our own life, period. But this leads to a semiexistence void of dreams, plans, and true joy—not honoring God by exploring our talents and abilities, not taking ownership for our own life, not really living. The danger of getting lulled into this half-living is that it lowers our standards. Suddenly we're willing to link lives with almost anyone with a pulse just to shake us out of our boredom.

My former roommate and I watched with dismay as one of her friends, Cara, got into a dubious marriage after dabbling in college and nannying. When neither of these seemed to work for her, she suddenly found what looked like an escape route from doing the difficult work of forging her own path in life. After an extremely short dating period, she got engaged to an out-of-state man ten years her senior who didn't share her faith and who didn't seem to treat her very nicely. But he did "save" her from her life of dabbling and disappointment and provide her with a path in life—wife and motherhood.

Getting Creative

On the flip side of Cara is Kate, a woman I met during a summer internship in D.C. She gave me one of the finest examples of not letting disappointment with life stop you from truly living. This single California girl and I kept in touch via letters and postcards for a couple years after our summer together in our nation's capital. My favorite postcard is the one she sent me from Italy. It said something about always wanting to go to Italy on her honeymoon and finally deciding to go for it when she reached her early thirties with no marriage prospects in sight. This gutsy gal was tackling Italy—and the ability of unmet expectations to lull us into a holding-pattern life—on her own. If there ever was a you-go-girl incident, this was it!

I know other women who've tackled life with similar single-girl gusto. Julie bought one of the cutest houses in our burb on her own. A single woman in my office adopted three kids—all from troubled backgrounds. My former roommate, Karen, found an ad in the back of a Christian magazine about a program where she could get her master's degree while teaching in Mongolia for two years. Oddly enough, she's fascinated with this land of yaks and cashmere, and with no hubby or kiddies to hold her back, she's heading out in a month. All of these single women will admit they thought life would turn out differently than it did. But I love that none of them sat around bemoaning their tough luck, waiting indefinitely for a man to come along so they could get a house, some kids, or ministry opportunities. Instead, they each devised an awesome Plan B to tackle.

From watching women such as these and from attempting to create my own Plan B, I've discovered one of the secrets to surviving unmet expectations: Change your expectations. Instead of thinking a husband, kids, and matching china are guarantees in life, we need to realize they're only one brand of the blessings God gives. When we take the blinders off and realize God wants to bless us and lead us in a whole bunch of different ways, not just down the domestic path, we're free to follow him with abandon and without disappointment. When we change our expectation from a life of being a wife and mom to a life of following God wherever he takes us, it's much more difficult to get disappointed. No longer do our life expectations hinge on outward, often uncontrollable factors (such as finding a person we want to spend the rest of our life with). Instead they're contingent on determination and devotion to God's leading.

I'd Carpe Diem, but . . .

This concept of changing our expectations and outlook sounds easy enough. However, there are a few fears that can get in the way.

I'll Be Single Forever!

Part of shifting our life expectations involves embracing our singleness. Doing this can seem scary on many levels. First of all, embracing anything involves a certain amount of commitment. And we find ourselves face-to-face with the fear that embracing our singleness means we're committing to it permanently. It's easier to put off the fear that resides deep in the heart of all of us single girls—that we'll grow old alone—if we put off single life altogether. Instead of taking advantage of the unique freedoms and blessings of singleness, we reside in a noncommittal holding-pattern life just outside the grasp of permanent singlehood. Or so we think. The irony is that a life half-lived isn't so attractive to most healthy, well-rounded potential mates. So in the end, we're stuck in that holding pattern, not moving toward marriage and not enjoying our singleness.

I'll Start Accumulating Cats!

Another scary thing is the stereotype of the single woman: She lives alone in her musty apartment with twenty-seven cats and is a crotchety old broad with a pinched face and gray hair pulled back in a tight bun. It's easy to think that embracing our singleness may put us on a no-turning-back road to becoming this nasty gal. Again, refusing to embrace our singleness can make us think we're putting off the risk of becoming the scary stereotype. But, to the contrary, all the single women I've known who have refused to be stalled by unmet expectations (even those who've dared to get cats!) and have regrouped and moved toward a full life—on their own—have found immense happiness.

I'll Have to Face the World Alone!

There's something about having someone next to us that makes it easier to face the world. For example, if we're with a friend in public and we trip, we can laugh together and walk on. But if we're alone in public and trip, laughing can seem kind of creepy and maniacal. When we're with someone and we see something cool, we can elbow the person and say, "Look at that!" But when you're alone, you either silently appreciate whatever's so cool or elbow strangers and risk creepiness again.

These are some of the reasons that kept me from venturing into public alone for many years of my singleness, but one of the things that pushed me into public sans partner was solo business trips. As I slowly and begrudgingly ventured out by myself, I learned that when I'm alone in public, I notice a lot more, have cool conversations with people I don't know, and see God's fingerprints a whole lot more often and more clearly.

Face Your Fears

Once we've named our unmet expectations and fears, we're free to stop running from them and allowing them to consciously or subconsciously control our life. The only way to do this is to face our fears head-on and then hand them over to the only one big enough to handle them: God. We may have to do this time and time again as these nasty fears and disappointments creep back into our life. But God will meet us with open arms every time we bring this "junk" back to him.

What's holding you back from embracing your singleness? Whatever it is, be honest with God about it and work on leaving it at the foot of the cross. Like me, I'm sure you'll find great delight in the fact that God gives beauty for ashes (Isa. 61:3). We give him our fears, shortcomings, disappointments, and anger, and he gives us forgiveness, a future, and hope (Jer. 29:11).

And while you're coming clean with God and ridding yourself of narrow expectations or neurotic fears about the future, together you and he can dream up some new, more realistic expectations for your life. What better person to do this with than the one who created you, wired you with gifts and abilities, and desires you to use these things to his and your delight? I know this much: He'll outdream us any day if we open our life and heart to him. Armed with his vision, we'll see that life not turning out as *we* thought it would can be an amazing blessing.

Three Reasons Why
Men Aren't the Enemy

*C*ontrary to the title of this chapter, I will admit there are numerous times when men FEEL like the enemy, times when they all seem like insensitive louts who were placed on this earth solely to manipulate our feelings and toy with our emotions. In all my vast, unofficial research—based on my own relationships and those of my friends—I've discovered that our anger toward men stems from a few common sources.

Top Three Reasons Why
We Think Men Are the Enemy

#1 They're Not Prince Charming

We grew up believing in fairy-tale men. Beauty had her Beast, Lady had her Tramp, Lois Lane had her Superman, Polly Purebred had her Underdog, and on . . . and on . . . and on. Each of these men was perfect in his own way. Beast wasn't just big and strong and kind of an intriguing "bad boy;" he was sensitive and caring. Superman didn't just have abs of steel; he was an entire man of steel who saved the planet, met deadlines, and looked hot in glasses. Whether we realized it or not, as children we were being groomed to think some superstud would one day come into our life, think we were wonderful, and be . . . well, perfect.

And then we grew up!

Once boys stopped seeming yucky and we actually gave them a second glance (I'll admit, for me this was sometime during kindergarten), we also realized that between moments of wonderfulness, they can also be mean, insensitive, and gross. They don't fight against dastardly foes for our safety and good name (sometimes they *are* our dastardly foes!). They aren't rugged and sensitive—often they're just unkempt. And they rarely recycle, let alone attempt to save the planet.

This is reality. We're forced to choose from among God's fallen creatures, creatures just as fallen as . . . us. The sooner we realize we aren't offering perfection (I'm no Polly Purebred, I don't know about you), the easier it is to accept that Mr. Perfect doesn't exist. The sooner we accept that Mr. Perfect doesn't exist, the sooner we can ditch our quest for this nonexistent "holy grail." And the sooner we quit this quest, the sooner we can get down to business—with real people, real expectations, and real relationships.

#2 They Don't Complete Us

I wish I could find the writers of the Tom Cruise blockbuster *Jerry McGuire* and give them a much-deserved whack upside the head. While the movie was fun and entertaining and gave us a rare glimpse of one of our favorite male specimens appearing endearingly geeky in a few scenes, it also gave us one of the worst lines in relationshipdom: "You complete me." I'll admit,

I was among the women in the audience who sighed dreamily when Tom uttered these words to girl-next-door Renee Zellwegger. It seemed like just about the most romantic thing a girl could hear her man say. Not just "I love you." Not just "I want to marry you." But "You have such great qualities and you and I fit together so well that you alone make me a whole person." *Sigh.*

This is part of the whole concept that two halves make a whole, that your spouse can be your "better half," that we aren't complete human beings until we've linked arms with someone for life. This can sound fine (we sure hear it a lot in subtle and not-so-subtle ways in TV shows, movies, and books), and there are a lot of people who ascribe to this theology of relationships. But when we take a step back and look at this line of thinking, we realize we've all been fed a bunch of hooey. When I look in my Bible, I don't read anything about God creating half-people. Instead, I see that God creates each of us in our mother's womb (Ps. 139:13), he saves us one by one when we choose to believe that his son died for the sake of our sins (John 3:16), and he equips us with gifts and abilities (Rom. 12:6–8). We were never meant to complete one another. Only God does that.

My friend Susan, who I first mentioned in chapter 9, has been like a poster child for the concept that men don't complete us. She and I enjoyed a casual friendship based on our shared faith, common hairdresser, similar taste in clothes,

Single Stuff

Even God Is Single (So Stop Giving Me a Hard Time)
by Karen Salmansohn

Dubbed "the book every single girl needs to defend against nudgy family and friends," this hip little tome offers twenty-six snappy comebacks to the mother-of-all singlehood questions: "Why aren't you married?" Flipping through it is like getting a pep talk from a cool, creative, slightly crass girlfriend.

and love of the show *Friends* . . . until one day about four months ago. It had been obvious for many weeks that something wasn't right with Susan. She'd lost a lot of weight from her already petite frame, and I often noticed the telltale signs that she'd been crying. During a private conversation one day, I finally asked, "Are you okay?" Instantly tears filled her eyes and she collapsed into a nearby chair. In between body-wracking sobs, she shared her suspicions that her husband of three months was having an affair. I wrapped my arms around her fragile body, stripped of weight from stress-induced loss of appetite and sleepless nights, and cried with her over unfulfilled dreams, unfair circumstances, and an uncertain future.

During this difficult time for Susan—filled with Christian counseling sessions, arguments and anger, good days and tearful days, two steps forward and three steps back—she's been told by nearly all the friends she's shared her struggles with to take good care of herself and to take time to do things that make her happy. It's her response to this advice that's broken my heart most. With tearful eyes and a defeated look, she whispered to me one day, "I don't know what makes me happy. I'm beginning to realize I don't really know who I am."

I was surprised by this admission. I'd always seen Susan as put together, friendly, responsible, and outgoing. But when she explained that she spent most of her and her husband's three-year dating relationship investing in his life and dreams, letting him pursue a degree while she put her work aspirations on hold, and how he's called the shots for everything from dinner decisions to money matters, I realized Susan had fallen into the common trap of losing herself for the sake of love. A trap I've nearly fallen into a few times myself.

I've watched friends get married because it was easier for them to walk down the aisle than to chart life's path or to dig deep and figure out just who it is God made them to be. I've fretted for some who married so young, becoming a "we" before they had much of a chance to figure out "me." I've thought about my own Mr. Close Enough, whom I begrudgingly walked away from in my early twenties, and wondered who I'd be now if I hadn't had to do the hard work of making some life decisions of my own over the past years.

I'm not saying that all who marry young are doomed or that all who marry at all are avoiding reality. Most assuredly, there are healthy, happy marriages in abundance. But there are also a lot of people getting hitched because it seems easier to become Wife or Husband (and soon after, Mom or Dad) than to do the difficult work of growing up and growing into the specific roles, ministries, paths, and professions to which God calls each of us.

It's also tempting for us single people to put our life on hold until we can assume the ready-made role of Wife. But in talking with Susan, I've realized afresh that the three little words many of us long to hear most—"I love you"—can be robbed of much of their richness and meaning when we haven't first asked ourselves a different, but just as vital, three little words—"Who am I?"

Susan's figuring out the hard way that two half-people don't make a whole, healthy marriage. And I'm still learning the hard way, too, that one half-person makes for a miserable single life. And anyway, God doesn't make half-people, and his promises don't come packaged for pairs. God completes us. Each of us. And it's only when we allow him to do so that we find true joy and the abundant life to which he's called us.

As for Susan, she's now taking some classes to help figure out what gives her—and God—joy. I love cheering her on as she comes into her own more and more. I hope someday in the future to be joined in this joy by her husband, as he realizes what a gem he's married to. Until then, I know God is guiding this caterpillar as she spins a cocoon, and I eagerly anticipate the day when she'll emerge a beautiful butterfly—whole, confident in God's love for her, and free to fly in the direction he beckons.

#3 They Don't Sweep Us Off Our Feet

A couple winters ago I found myself at the end of the work-day, sweeping snow off my car. Carla, a coworker of mine, was doing the same in the parking space next to mine. This being toward the end of our long Chicago winter, it felt like the 257th time I'd swept snow off my poor little car that month. I could tell Carla shared my winter weariness, so hoping a little levity would help, I said, "You know, this is one of the three main reasons I want a husband. Scraping ice and snow off my car, killing bugs, and balancing my checkbook. I don't think that's too much to ask, do you?" This married woman and I shared a laugh, then she said something I'll always remember: "Some days having someone to scrape ice off your car is the best thing you get out of the bargain." We shared another laugh, but I tucked this important truth in the back of my brain. I knew Carla—and her great relationship with her husband, Jimmy—well enough to know she wasn't husband-bashing. She was just pointing out the fact that marriage isn't all romance and hot sex.

I've heard other happily married women second this truth in various ways over the years. They've talked about the unique sounds and smells husbands have introduced to their world. One woman spoke of waking up on the first morning of her honeymoon to find her husband not totally enthralled with her unparalleled beauty as she'd dreamed, but buying baseball cards over the phone from the Home Shopping Network, which he was watching on the hotel's television. Author and marriage therapist Leslie Parrott talks about being initially disillusioned at the relative unromanticness of real-life marriage—and about reworking her expectations. She stumbled upon what she calls the "sacrament of the ordinary," or taking delight in the little things of marriage, such as sharing a belly laugh or a walk in the rain. Most days this is as good as marriage gets. And all these married women will testify that once you adjust your expectations away from grandiose expressions of love, most days the little things are more than enough. So getting fixated on flowers and love poems now only sets us up for disappointment later.

I got "swept off my feet" once by a guy I dated in college. He gave me candy, stuffed animals, flowers, and gushy cards all within the first couple weeks of getting to know one another. Though on some levels it was sweet and exciting, I remember how artificial it felt to be showered with gifts that had more to do with his "dating script" than with who I was. I felt like I could have been any girl and he'd have reacted with the exact same succession of gifts. The whole experience left me feeling rather empty. Maybe being swept off our feet is overrated. Anyway, I suspect our desire for this romantic ideal stems more from our wish to have a great story to tell our girlfriends (and grandchildren!) than from wanting to launch into a long-term, healthy relationship.

In the end, it seems most of our anger and disillusionment with men stem from our erroneous expectations. Life isn't a fairy tale or a well-scripted chick flick, and when we let men off the hook for not living up to these fictional ideals, we're finally ready for real-life love.

Male Bashing—
And Other Guilty Pleasures

*O*bviously there are myriad other reasons we think men are the enemy besides the three mentioned in the last chapter. I can think of a few examples from my own dating escapades: The guy I dated in college whose rampant sense of humor was often at my expense—leaving my budding self-esteem in shambles. The guy from a Bible study I was in who would talk with me on the phone for four hours at a time and sing love songs to me in his car, but then would swear we were "just friends." And the guy who broke up with me in the parking lot at an out-of-state Christian music festival we were attending with a bunch of mutual friends—on my birthday, no less!

On a side note: I know many of you have stories of guys treating you much worse than my dating mishaps. I can't state strongly enough that there's absolutely no excuse for abuse—

either verbal or physical—of any kind. One of the reasons I advocate strong, full-bodied singlehood is that it helps women realize that being alone—no matter how difficult it may be some days—is so much better than being with someone who's all wrong or even dangerous for you.

But for many of us, the temptation isn't so much to stay in bad relationships as to hold on to grudges for all the nicks and dings we've suffered from relational mismatches along the way. I'll admit, these grudges can seem awfully great at times. They provide "company" when the men who inspired them are long gone. They offer splendid (albeit erroneous) reasons for being alone—"Just look at all the louts I've dated—all the good men are taken!" They can become a panacea of sorts for the sting of rejection—since it was all *his* fault, after all! And, best of all, they can provide great stories at single-girl get-togethers!

The Ketchup Queen

There's a scenario that repeats itself every now and then when I'm out with friends. Someone orders a dish that comes with fries, she struggles with the ketchup bottle, and I brag that I know the secret of extracting this condiment from its stubborn container. I valiantly take the bottle and (read closely now!) hit the neck hard with the heel of my hand. Then I smile widely as the red stuff flows freely on my friend's plate.

"Where'd you learn that?" someone inevitably asks, to which I always respond, "I learned that from an old boyfriend. It's hands-down the best thing I got out of the relationship." Then we all laugh, and occasionally launch into ex-boyfriend bashing.

Let's face it, those of us who've been single for a number of years have experienced more than our fair share of pain and rejection at the hands of those we cared about, whether they meant to hurt us or not.

My friends and I often laugh about The Fence Breaker, the guy who drove into my friend Julie's fence when he went to pick her up for a date. To make matters worse, he never made good on his promise to fix it. Every now and then I remind another friend that she deserves someone so much better than her ex. He had more issues than the magazine section of Borders, yet he dragged *her* into counseling for a little "fixing up."

While these hurtful behaviors are so easy to see, what's harder to glimpse is the good in our exes. And it's there, whether we want to admit it or not. No matter how someone may have treated us, he's still one of God's creations.

Convicted by my funny yet not-so-Christlike words recently, I started trying to see the good qualities in my exes, the things that drew me to them in the first place. With God's help I've come to realize the guy who undermined my self-esteem with his constant sarcastic comments also helped birth my love for travel. And the old flame who broke my heart by dumping me on my birthday also made me feel beautiful for the first time in my life. Seeing the good in these guys, savoring the great memories of our time together, and thanking God for the positives amidst the negatives has led me to a less jaded, more hopeful outlook. And one that pleases God.

Don't get me wrong. I'm not making excuses for hurtful behavior. But as pastor and author Lee Strobel once wrote, "Bitter, angry people don't hold a grudge as much as the grudge holds them." Looking for the good in a past relationship may seem a Pollyannalike exercise, but it yields amazing benefits: happier, healthier singlehood.

So the next time I'm the ketchup hero at dinner with friends, I'll simply say, "I learned that trick from an old boyfriend. He was really handy like that." I may miss a good laugh, but we'll all gain a more positive perspective on the opposite gender, relationships, and this strange world of singleness.

I Love My Attitude Problem

When we take an honest look at the grudges we allow ourselves to hang on to, we realize how unbiblical—and ugly—they are. Admit it, right after your fear of never finding the love of your life lies the sheer terror of turning into the stereotype of a bitter old spinster who's angry at the world (including her twenty-seven cats!). Since anger only seems to grow and build upon itself, eventually giving way to bitterness and crotchety-ness, holding a grudge against a guy (or two, or three . . .) only takes us one step closer to scary spinsterhood.

I'll admit it can be empowering to hold on to a grudge—especially if a relationship was ripped from you without any input or warning. If you weren't allowed the choice to hang on to the relationship, the choice to hang on to a grudge can seem awfully tempting, like it's your only chance at power in an otherwise powerless situation.

And it seems the older we get and the longer the dry spells between dates—let alone dating relationships—last, the easier it is to feel angry at the whole male gender. When we were growing up, a mate seemed like a guarantee, right up there with growing taller and finally being able to "get" all those things we were told "you'll understand when you're older." So when that guarantee of a mate, that long-held dream, doesn't come true like we'd hoped, the logical response is to feel ripped-off and angry. And the "logical" people with whom to get angry are men. We get angry at our exes for not finding us wife-worthy—or for not being our particular brand of "knight in shining armor." And we get angry at men in general for not asking us out for years on end. (And even a little angry at our parents, extended families, churches, and culture for offering us an untrue paradigm for the future.)

The Vicious Cycle

But as tempting and easy to justify as this anger can seem, when it takes up residency and grows within us, it only makes us bitter, nasty people. Not exactly the kind of women who attract men—at least healthy, nonmasochistic ones. That unattractive attitude within us only repels relationships, leaving us feeling even more overlooked, cheated, and frustrated. Which only makes us that much more angry and unattractive. And so the cycle begins . . . and continues . . . ad nauseum.

Or until we finally remember God's commands about forgiveness. It's amazing how easy it is to forget how forgiven we are and how much forgiveness is required of us in multiple verses throughout the Bible. In Matthew 18:21, Peter asks Jesus how many times we're required to forgive those who wrong us. "Up to seven times?" he asks, no doubt thinking this is generous. Jesus' response sets the bar a lot higher than most of us wronged humans (read: all of us) want to hear: "I tell you, not seven times, but seventy-seven times" (Matt. 18:22). The parables he then tells in Matthew 23–25 illustrate how God forgives us to the extent that we forgive others. Kind of puts our grudges in a whole new light, doesn't it? Ephesians 4:32 and Colossians 3:13 both instruct us to forgive others just as we are forgiven. Which brings up a good point: We hurt, disappoint, manipulate, pigeonhole, steamroll, and otherwise damage men just as much as they do us. We need their forgiveness just as much as they need ours. When I take an honest look back at the men I've dated, I realize I've subjected them to PMS attacks, angry outbursts, humor at their expense, neglect, and . . . well, you get the idea. Men are not Prince Charmings, and we aren't exactly princesses ourselves. So accusing them of being less than perfect is kind of like the pot calling the kettle black.

Opportunities for grudges, male bashing, and angry outbursts are rampant in our tell-all, sue-all society. But please, oh please, work with me with all your might to resist these temptations. I know firsthand that giving in only makes us, everyone around us, and the God who created us, miserable. Then we aren't such great representatives of the God of all love, and we have a distorted image of him, since he's our heavenly *Father* and the Son of *Man.*

Besides prayer and divine intervention, another antidote I've discovered to combat bad attitudes toward men is having male friends.

Friends with Testosterone

Thankfully, male presence in our life doesn't have to be all or nothing. I'm grateful for the guys I'm privileged to call friends; they have enriched my life in so many ways and have helped fill the husband-sized hole I sometimes feel in my life. Take a look around you and see if these guys exist in your life—or at least the potential for some of these guys. Finding and cultivating these friendships can help keep loneliness, anger, and unrealistic expectations at bay.

The Brother

Tim, a married coworker of mine, has been a combination of friend, tech support, and matchmaker in my life. I enjoy hanging out with him and his wife, Michelle, playing guys-against-girls card games with them and another one of Tim's friends. When I needed to buy a computer, Michelle graciously lent Tim to me for an afternoon of shopping that went way over my head and left Tim in techie heaven. And Tim (with Michelle's watchful yea or nay) has set me up with a couple of his old college buddies for casual foursome evenings out and even for the ever-dreaded company Christmas party. When Tim stops by my office (usually to borrow money for the pop machine), he asks about my latest dating endeavors, dispensing brotherly advice (usually calling my latest love interest "monkey boy") and reminding me "he who wait for perfect horse has mighty long walk" (which I think is his fortune-cookie way of reminding me nobody's perfect).

Maybe you have a biological brother who plays this role, or just a good guy friend. But having someone to look out for you, check out your love interests from a male perspective, and dispense brotherly advice can help you stay grounded, realistic, and protected.

Single Stuff

www.osolomio.com

This travel group serves those who want to see the world but don't necessarily have someone to see it with. Their domestic and international excursions allow you to make the most of your single freedom—and make some new friends in the process (they stress that this isn't a dating service).

The Handyman

Shawn, my former roommate's brother-in-law (did you follow all that?), is almost more a friend to my car than to me. He's a mechanic and changes my oil at his home for a mere ten dollars—all while I watch his cable television, chat with his wife, or play with his baby. When I moved several months ago, he went with me to rent the moving truck and drove it to and from my old and new apartments. Shawn's saved me more money on car repairs over the years than I can count and has introduced the phrase "right CV boot" into my vocabulary (though all I know is it's an expensive car part!). My friend Julie's handyman guy friend is Bob, who helps with home repairs that call for more than her strength or selection of tools—and that usually involve crawling up on her roof.

No matter how independent we may be, things are going to come up that require skills and strength that typically require more testosterone than we possess. Having a handyman friend to call when you need a window air conditioner unit installed, a couch moved, or a toilet repaired can save you money, a hernia, and feelings of helplessness.

The Dreamer

Ray is a guy friend I met at a singles Bible study ages ago. For years, he, my old roommate, and I were the social committee of our group—us girls would buy the food and decor and Ray would open up his big ol' bachelor pad for our shindigs. After everyone would leave, the three of us would sit around and talk about God and our dreams and the future. Ray was one of the first people to challenge me to write a book, and years later he followed his own go-big-or-stay-home advice and quit his corporate-jungle job to attend a Bible college in Sweden. Just the other day this friend called me from Paris (because he knows I'm a Paris-loving freak), where he's seeing the sights with some random young couple. Ray's been a great example of living large and seizing the day—and we all need this kind of nudge in our life from time to time.

For lack of someone to dream with about your combined future, it's nice to have a guy who'll let you dream about your own future—and who'll cheer you on and believe in you no matter what.

The Martian

I originally mentioned Max, a musician friend I met through work, in chapter ten. He's the one I interact with via phone since we live at opposite ends of the Chicagoland area. Though I treasure his unconditional friendship and encouragement of my artistic endeavors, our sitcomlike conversations have been like a case study for the whole Mars/Venus thing. Many times I've called him for moral support and instead received helpful hints on how to solve my problem du jour (very sweet, but NOT what I was looking for!). Other times I've sought his advice, only to realize how differently men and women approach relationships, work woes, and just life in general. My friendship with Max has helped me to appreciate the differences between men and women, to realize that expecting a man to play a female friend's role in my life will leave me unhappy every time, and to enjoy the wonderfully unique role he plays in my life.

Having a martian friend will help you get a handle on people with Y chromosomes and will help you retain realistic expectations for this species.

Having a few positive male relationships in our life can go a long way toward helping us realize that guys are human beings just like us, in need of patience, humor, forgiveness, celebration, and meaningful relationships. When we decide to stop holding over their heads the ways they've wronged us and to refuse to degenerate into card-carrying male bashers, we're finally free to have healthy relationships with the opposite sex. These friends will help fill our need for male interaction, and maybe some day one of these guys will even vow to be our best friend 'til death do us part.

Bad Boys—
Whatcha Gonna Do
When They Come for You?

hen we hold grudges against men, it can cloud our thinking. Unchecked anger and frustration can lead us to give up our quest for a healthy relationship by seeking an easy way out or by lowering our expectations. If you're currently "up to here" with dating-game frustration or loneliness woes, be wary of these guys.

Mr. Right Now

Recently my friend Margaret told me about some friends who wigged out when they hit a certain age and were still single. We've all seen it—someone who hits the wall in her single journey and suddenly says something akin to "I'm going to marry the next man who walks through that door." As soon as someone with a pulse shows the least amount of interest in her, she's engaged. Though we still celebrate her upcoming nuptials with showers and oohs and ahs, we know deep inside that 'til death do us part is going to be a long, arduous journey for this couple whose main motivation for marrying is avoiding dateless Friday nights. But all it takes is one conversation with someone who married a Mr. Right Now to realize that dateless Friday nights are far better than a lifetime of miserable Friday nights married to a mismatch. Don't let timing be your main motivator for getting into a relationship or getting hitched. Married forty-year-olds can be just as miserable—sometimes more so—than still single forty-year-olds.

I heard a wonderful story recently about a woman who married for the first time at fifty-five. Fifty-five! While she'd wanted to get married all along, she held out for someone worth spending the rest of her life with. She's now happy as a clam. And if she'd married a Mr. Right Now along the way, she would have missed this opportunity at genuine marital bliss. She's glad she waited. You will be, too.

Mr. Close Enough

After a certain amount of time, it's easy to lower your standards. If the stretches between dating relationships gets longer and longer each time, you can get lulled into thinking that eventually that next shot won't come. And when the pool of available men gets smaller over the years, you may find that guys who are only a semi-good match for you look amazing. But just because there may be enough good qualities in a guy to pull you into a dating relationship, that doesn't necessarily mean there are enough good qualities to make him your lifelong companion. This one's really tough. There's a fine line between a good guy and a good-for-you guy. Holding out for the latter is super. Going for the former is settling.

I know firsthand how gut-wrenching it can be to walk away from a Mr. Close Enough. I've done it myself, and it took all kinds of prayer, friend support, time, and Edy's Grand Light French Silk ice cream to get over it. There can be what-ifs for years, and you may even get back together a time or two. But this is when being in constant contact with God is crucial. He'll help you realize the difference between cold feet, which is normal, and God's "no," which is usually accompanied by a constant lack of peace about joining your life with this guy's (at least that was my experience). If you know the guy you're dating is good, but not good enough to be a keeper for you, get out fast. The longer you stay in the relationship, the more difficult good-bye will be, and the more tempted you'll be to settle for less than God's best. Just keep repeating to yourself, "This is the rest of my life we're dealing with here," and, "It's better to be single and lonely than married and miserable."

Mr. Wrong

When relationships with Christian guys don't work out time after time, guys who don't share our faith can take on a new allure. Besides that whole good-girl/bad-boy attraction, there's the sheer numbers to consider. Narrowing our selection to those who are Christians makes the pool pretty small. Weed out guys who still live at home at thirty-five, who have odd attachments to their mothers or their pets, or who have addictions or major unresolved issues, and there's barely enough guys for you and me. That can make us dangerously vulnerable to someone who's flat-out wrong for us. Take a clue from my near miss.

The Allure of Mr. Wrong

It's ironic that I met Jake at a church, considering my main reservation about him is his lack of Christian faith and values. But that's where it all started—in a church sanctuary at a friend's wedding. During the slower parts of the service, I did my usual scan of the crowd for cute, seemingly unattached guys. In his dark suit and preppy glasses, Jake definitely caught my attention. I quickly put together that he was a friend of some friends of mine and was pleased when he sat down next to me at the reception.

Sitting there in the church basement with friends and family, I enjoyed chatting with this funny, talkative, well-dressed guy. In this context, his occasional swearing and drinking binges with "the boys" didn't come up. He was just charming—even the parent-types at the table seemed to think he was great. So when he asked if he could call me sometime, I did a mental dance of joy and gave him my number.

The next time I saw him was at the house of one of our mutual friends. Over dinner, the guys swapped stories about the stupid things they'd done while drunk, including nearly getting in trouble with the law. Although I knew they were exaggerating a bit to impress and/or shock us girls, I still should have been turned off. But for some inexplicable reason (other than the whole good-girl/bad-boy attraction), I was still a bit intrigued. The clincher was several days later when Jake called and asked me to meet him for coffee. It was a last-minute thing and I almost didn't go. But I'm a Starbucks junkie and was touched by the thoughtful invite, considering he doesn't even drink coffee (and knows I love it). So I went, and one-on-one I discovered Jake is very intelligent, devoted to his family, and easy to talk to. But—not a Christian.

That realization should have put an end to my attraction. But I admit I was drawn by Jake's interest in me. He was one of the "cool kids," a type who, up until then, hadn't seemed to notice I was alive. Here was a tall, dark, handsome specimen of the popular crowd showing interest in goody-two-shoes me! Responding to his advances seemed like my duty to unnoticed good girls everywhere.

In the weeks and months that followed, Jake and I exchanged fun and flirty e-mails and hung out with his friends on occasion. When the conversation would turn to drinking or their love of going to Hooters, I would become silent or roll my eyes and offer a girl-power speech about women not being objects—failing to mention, unfortunately, that our value comes from being made in God's image. I think they were more amused than convinced by my occasional ranting, as the conversation would usually give way to teasing arguments and laughter.

I'd thought all this hanging out was harmless fun and maybe even God's answer to my prayer for more non-Christian friends with whom to share my faith. That is, until Jake asked me to join him and his family and friends for a weekend out of state at a rented beach house. I was flattered but caught off guard. Suddenly this wasn't so casual anymore. I could tell we were at a crossroads in our relationship—saying yes and going with him would definitely bring us closer together.

Faced with the decision of whether or not to go, I finally asked a few Christian friends for advice. Maggie, a church friend and hopeless romantic, suggested that spending a whole weekend together would finally give me the chance to discuss deeper matters of faith. Yet somehow I had the feeling the weekend would be less "Kum-ba-yah" and more keg city. Max, my best guy friend, told me to run as fast as I could in the other direction—not just from the invite, but from Jake in general. I saw his point, but also wondered what this would communicate about God's unconditional love for all people, especially those who don't yet know him.

I figured I needed more info to make the right decision and sent a breezy e-mail asking Jake about the sleeping arrangements and whether or not he thought there would be drinking over the weekend. His reply said there might be some drinking, but that I wouldn't have to be involved. He also included a flirty remark about where I could sleep. From what I knew of him, I was pretty certain this was a joke. But pretty certain wasn't good enough for a topic that's so serious to me. I knew sex before marriage is a no-go for me but couldn't assume Jake would jump to this conclusion for someone he simply knew to be a "good girl." Suddenly, the seemingly less exciting Christian guys I'd dated in the past became a lot more desirable. I hadn't realized how great it was to know we were on the same page when it came to Christian morals and beliefs.

I sent Jake another e-mail to make certain he knew where I stood on the sleeping arrangement situation. I wrote something about not wanting to seem square, but that I wanted to avoid any potentially awkward situations by making sure up front that he knew I have pretty conservative beliefs. His message back assured me he was indeed joking, that I'd have a bed to myself all week-

Single Stuff

"I Will Survive"
by Gloria Gaynor

This song is a kickin' reminder that though a relationship may be over, life isn't. Crank it up, sing it out, and move forward a stronger, wiser woman.

end, and that he appreciated my conservative views. "It's part of what makes you YOU," he wrote with a smiley face next to it. Reading that made me both giddy with the excitement of having someone interested in me and guilty that he didn't know the biggest part of what makes me me: Jesus Christ.

It was when I had dinner with Kate, a friend from church, that I finally made a decision about the weekend invite—and Jake. As we were eating, I filled her in on my growing relationship and the invite to the beach house. Usually one of my biggest cheerleaders, Kate listened quietly to my whole explanation, then paused thoughtfully for a moment. "You know, I'm glad you finally brought up this whole Jake thing," she said. "I've been worried about you for some time."

Really? Now it was my turn to listen intently.

"What are you doing with this Jake guy? You know he's not a Christian, right? You can say it's casual, but I see your face light up when you talk about him," she said as my face now grew red with the embarrassment of having the truth—which I'd previously denied to others and myself—laid bare. "He's not worth it. He's not worth YOU."

In the silent moments that followed, I finally faced a whole lot of truth. I had been fooling myself when I'd said our relationship was only casual. I was attracted to Jake and falling more and more with each interaction, flirtation, or teasing e-mail. And his recent e-mails confirmed that he was interested in more than friendship, too. I also realized that most of my attraction had been to his attention and flattery. It had been a while since anyone had shown interest in me, and the last guy I'd dated, though a Christian, had been really passive in his pursuit of our relationship. Jake's e-mails, in which he'd been open about his attraction to me, had been refreshing. And also, I now realized, a means of playing with fire.

I'd known all along what the Bible says about being involved with those who don't know Jesus. I'd read 2 Corinthians 6:14— "Do not be yoked together with unbelievers"—many times during Bible studies and sermons over the years. And I'd seen a few of my Christian friends date non-Christians and then suddenly disappear from church—and even start making a few lifestyle choices they previously wouldn't have dreamed of. I should have known better than to fall for Jake. And that was the most difficult truth to swallow.

I thanked Kate for her honesty and for holding me accountable and asked her to check up on me in the weeks and months ahead. After dinner I had a long talk with God in which I apologized for boosting my self-esteem with the wrong source—a guy instead of him. I asked for direction and realized, looking back, that he'd been giving it all along. Three different times over the previous months when I'd tried to get together with Jake one-on-one, something—or Someone—had forced us to cancel our plans at the last minute. God had been protecting my heart. And it was time for me to join him.

I also realized Jake needed God way more than he needed me. Part of his attraction to me undoubtedly had been an unconscious attraction to Jesus in me, and I didn't want to squelch that. Completely calling it quits on our relationship seemed too extreme a measure, like I was cutting off one of God's potential avenues of reaching Jake. I needed to do some careful finessing to keep our relationship casual and "just friends," but I didn't want my first flat-out talk about God to be in a disappointing light or to make him seem like a killjoy. Thankfully, before calling Jake to tell him I couldn't make the trip, I realized I was going to an out-of-state conference the weekend after the one he was asking about. I could honestly tell him that being out of town two weekends in a row would be too much. I could hear disappointment in his voice; I think he knew I was making a conscious choice about our relationship, that at this crossroads I was choosing friendship. When the time comes, I'll fill him in on all the reasoning behind this decision.

Since then our e-mails have been fewer and free of flirtation. I miss the rush of potential romance but have felt freer to tell Jake about all aspects of my life—including church activities and decisions driven by my faith—now that I'm not so concerned about what he thinks about me. I've asked Kate to keep me accountable to our mutual faith in God, to ask those difficult yet necessary questions about my motives and my heart when it comes to Jake. And I've sought to strengthen my security and self-worth by spending more quality time in prayer and Bible study, hopefully making me less susceptible to similar temptation in the future.

When it comes down to it, what Jake and I both need most is God. That's the most important common ground we share.

Take It or Leave It Love

In the end, successful singleness is found in creating such a great single life that only God's best for our life can pry us away from it. A man shouldn't be our escape or savior; he should be a bonus and companion. And somewhere between waiting for a prince to ride up on a white horse and sweep us away and looking for someone who's simply single and breathing is a healthy, balanced perspective.

It makes me think of Ron, the senior pastor at my church, who recently bought a car. He went in to talk to a dealer, knowing exactly what he wanted to spend. When the car salesman told him he couldn't go that low, Ron started to walk away. After a few moments, the salesman called after him and gave Ron the deal he'd asked for. I'm not sure this analogy completely fits; I certainly don't mean to objectify men. But I love the concept that Ron got what he wanted only when he was willing to walk away. I think that's how we need to be. It may take visiting a lot of dealerships. Or spending a lot of years just walking or taking the bus. But these things are better than getting stuck with a lemon any day.

Going Solo

*O*kay, so we've made peace with our family, our church, and the male gender. We've created a family of friends and revised our life expectations. And we know we're valuable in God's eyes—just as we are. These concepts sound great for today, next month, even next year. But will they fly ten or twenty years from now if we're still single? The answer: Only if we make some strategic plans for the future.

I hope that by now we can think about still being single ten or twenty years from now without hyperventilating or jumping off the nearest bridge. Once we accept the possibility that we may hit our next milestone birthday—or two—alone, we can make some concrete plans to ensure that the best is yet to come, no matter what our life looks like decades from now.

Dream Big

One of the best things anyone's advised me to do for my health as a single woman is to create "Have, Be, and Do" lists. Grab three pieces of paper and jot "Have" at the top of one, "Be" at the top of another, and "Do" at the top of the third. Then on the first sheet, jot down all the things you'd like to have someday. These things can be tangible, such as the "cool couch with legs" I jotted on my Have list, or intangible, such as "a healthy, happy marriage." These things aren't necessarily logical, and the sky's the limit. The point here is to get your dreams—all of them, not just the ones involving a spouse or children—on paper.

Once you've got a pretty good Have list going, switch to your Be list. What would you like to be today or someday? An accomplished pianist? A Proverbs-31-type woman? A great mom or great cook? Write it all down. Then move on to your Do list. Obviously, this is for things you'd like to do at some point in your life. My Do list contains things as diverse as go to Maine in autumn, send my parents on a trip to Canada (something they've long wanted to do), learn how to take decent pictures, and read straight through the entire Bible. Tap into the hidden dreams in your heart and jot them on your Do list.

Single Stuff

www.ccci.org/solo/

This is the Web home of SOLO (Singles Offering Life to Others), an interdenominational singles ministry from Campus Crusade for Christ that's focused on the unique aspects of being a single Christian in today's society. These single folks want to see God make a difference in their own lives and in the lives of others as they reach out with Christ's love.

What I love about this exercise is that it puts the desires of getting married and having kids in the context of all our dreams. It shows us that marriage isn't the end-all, beat-all accomplishment in life—nor is it the only desire God's planted in our heart. This exercise also provides a road map of sorts for the future. Whether or not we get married and whether or not our life turns out the way we think it will, if we refer back to these lists and pick goals from among them on a regular basis, we're guaranteed to have a vibrant, growing, risk-taking kind of life—one that honors all the gifts, abilities, and dreams God's wired in us.

Flying Solo

When I crossed one of the things off my Do list—go to Paris—I also found a new passion: travel. And this new passion has been a wonderful perk—and teacher—for me and several of my single friends. Traveling to other lands has been a liberating way to make the most of the unique freedoms of our singleness and has given us something else to discuss with others in lieu of a boyfriend or mate. I love that now whenever I see faraway family and friends, they ask about my latest adventures instead of recent (or nonexistent) dating escapades. I've been transformed from pitiable single girl to enviable adventuress.

In fact, my first—and hopefully not last—trip to Paris was solo. Not exactly the romantic adventure I'd long dreamed of. My European vacation began with an eight-hour plane ride—smashed between two couples—to visit my friend Christa, whose husband is a military man stationed in Germany. I somehow made my way through customs (after first waiting in the wrong line) and eventually found the baggage claim area in the Frankfurt airport, which is roughly the size of the town I grew up in. "I'm a grown woman, I can do this," I kept repeating to myself under my breath, feeling very small and alone in the sea of foreign faces. But I managed just fine.

Christa and I had planned to take a two-day bus tour of Paris. But her sudden morning sickness made the mere thought of the journey send her stomach into somersaults. "Wanna go with a friend of mine instead?" she offered. Well, at least Plan B sure beat going completely alone—or not going at all.

So a couple days later I boarded the German equivalent of a Greyhound Bus with Cherie, another military wife and friend of Christa's. We rode through the night, attempting to sleep in an upright position, with a busload of vacationing military personnel and their visiting friends and family.

We arrived in the City of Light at an insanely early hour and filed off the bus and into a café for a typical French breakfast—juice, coffee, and a small crusty croissant. We were sleepy, sticky, and sore after a night on the bus—and still hungry after our petite introduction to the gastronomic offerings of France. Not exactly the romantic trip to Paris I'd dreamed of over the years (walking hand-in-hand with my beret-wearing beau along the bank of the Seine). In reality, it was single ol' me and a busload of strangers.

But as the coffee kicked in and the day wore on, a wonderful vacation unfolded. I got to know Cherie, a neat sister in Christ. I went in with a couple of other women in our tour to purchase some Parisian perfume at a group discount. A military man from D.C. who was in our group helped Cherie and me navigate our way through the Louvre. And my favorite moment of the trip was when four of us ventured out after the planned events of the day and found a sidewalk café. There, in view of the Eiffel Tower, I sat sipping cappuccinos with three people I'd known for a whopping twenty-four hours. I caught these transplanted Americans up on trends in the U.S. while they told me fascinating tales of their adventures of work and play.

So my vacation photos contain me and a bunch of people I'll probably never see again. So my first glimpse of some of the most famous monuments in the world was shared with people who today probably don't remember my name. So what? I was in Paris! And my heart was stirred—no, not for a tall, dark, handsome man named Jean-Luc, but for a breathtaking city. And for a God who can orchestrate such surprising moments of singlehood joy.

Who knows, maybe someday if there's a husband in God's plan for me, we'll venture to Paris together, and I'll get to say,

"Honey, here's where what's-her-name and I caught our first glimpse of the Eiffel Tower!"

Table for One

On a smaller scale, I've also learned the joy of venturing into public alone. At first this seemed scary and creepy, and I didn't try it willingly. It was only when circumstances (being in another state for work and not wanting to spend all my evenings cooped up in my hotel room) forced me out by myself that I realized how uniquely enjoyable this could be.

For example, the first and only Broadway play I've ever seen I attended alone. I was in New York for a conference, and after spending the first night in my hotel room relishing room service and cable television from the vast expanse of my king-size bed, I mustered the courage to take in New York the next night. After conferring with the concierge, hitting the Hot Tix booth at nearby Times Square, and asking a grandfatherly man for directions to the theater, I stood in the foyer with all the other tourists waiting for the theater to begin seating for *Cats*.

While all the other patrons of the arts chatted amongst themselves, I snuck in some inconspicuous people watching (one of my favorite pastimes), then stared at the ceiling, the walls, and the floor as time dragged on and on. I wondered if I looked as awkward as I felt, standing there alone amongst all the happy chatter.

When the ushers finally let us in, I took my plush aisle seat and was happy to find myself next to a family of five, instead of sticking out like a sore thumb in my own row. During the intermission I even struck up a conversation with the woman next to me, the mom of the family, and discovered the family was from Denmark and was on their first trip to the States. We had a delightful conversation as she told me of all the wonderful sites they'd seen—until the lights dimmed and the singing, dancing cat-people reappeared.

Walking back to the hotel after the show, I realized I probably wouldn't have had that conversation—and probably wouldn't have taken the time to admire the theater's beautiful architecture—had I been there with people I knew. Maybe venturing alone in public wasn't as bad as I'd previously thought.

Since then, I've eaten alone in restaurants and gone to see movies alone, both away from home on business trips and in my own neighborhood. Each time, I marvel at the conversations, observations, and opportunities I probably would have missed if I hadn't been alone. And each time I care a little less what others think about my aloneness and learn to enjoy my own company a bit more. I laugh a little louder and see a whole lot more—including those easy-to-miss moments of God's grace.

Prior to my solo excursions, I erroneously thought being lonely and being alone were synonymous. Now I know better. I would even suggest that we need to learn to enjoy and be comfortable with our own company before we truly can be good company for anyone else.

Don't get me wrong. I still love hanging out with my friends; they just aren't a prerequisite for fun anymore. And there are still the occasional awkward moments when I'm out alone, but I'm learning to ask God to fill them with his surprise blessings and to use those silences to help me tune in to his still, small voice. Though aloneness isn't always on our agenda, sometimes I suspect it's part of God's grand plan to get our attention and remind us that no matter where we are or whom we're with (or without), he's always there.

There's No Place like Home

One of the easiest places for us single girls to put life on hold is in our own home. Buying furniture, dishes, or even a house can be financially difficult for a single woman, but I'd venture a guess that just as often it's our own hang-ups that prevent us from acquiring these things. We're stalled by the thought that we're supposed to register for dishes, not select, save up, and buy them alone. We're hesitant to buy furniture just for us. We're hung up on the vision of house hunting with a spouse, not as a solo endeavor. And so we remain with hand-me-down furniture we don't necessarily like in an apartment that has a very temporary feel.

I moved into my first solo apartment a year ago, and in this space that was all mine, I spread out, I decorated, I created a *home*. Though my one-bedroom home is sans dishwasher, washer/dryer, and central air, it now sports telltale signs of me: some sort of Eiffel Tower in every room, vintage magazine covers on the walls, antique furniture I've refinished myself, more books than I could ever read, and my quirky collection of pitchers. My humble abode might not be much, but it's *me*. And for that, I love it. I love returning home to a place that's such an expression of my passions. I love hanging out there in my pajamas, eating ice cream out of the carton while watching my latest Blockbuster selection—all by myself. I love that being alone in my home is fun and comforting, so much so that I sometimes break into the I-love-living-alone dance (don't laugh, I know some of you do this too!).

One of my heroes is my dear friend Julie. She bought a house by herself several years ago and has furnished it with a homey combo of folk art, Polish pottery, and photos of her growing number of nieces and nephews. She regularly invites The Girls and me and other friends and family over for parties, barbeques, and her annual Christmas soiree. Recently, as she was talking about her massive garden, her latest home repairs, and her renovation plans, I said to her in a tone that was half-complimentary and half-teasing, "You're such a grown-up!" We laughed, and I filed away in my mind my admiration for a single person who's fully invested in life. I admire her flair and willingness to practice hospitality despite the fact she— as a thirtysomething single woman—isn't your typical Susie Homemaker.

Julie and I and many of our single friends have learned the joy of creating a home *now* with whatever resources we have. Doing so has made our current status a lot more enjoyable. What's great is that it's possible to establish a home in a studio or a three-bedroom house, with flea-market furniture or an entire Pottery Barn spread. The key ingredient is our heart. Once we tap into that and allow it expression, our lives—and our homes—can be wonderful places to dwell.

Where Do We Go from Here?

*L*et's be honest. Even when we tap into our dreams, establish a home, learn to enjoy our own company, and experience the joy of going solo, there are still days when being single stinks.

As much as I love being single and try to eke out every ounce of joie de vivre this life station offers, there are moments when loneliness launches a surprise attack and threatens to overtake me. It comes at random moments—when I see a couple exchange a loving glance, when I'm sitting alone at church in a sea of happy families, when I'm having my 237th straight Girls Night. It's the "One of These Things Is Not Like the Other" syndrome that strikes when everyone else at work is talking about their spouse—except me. It's that little voice in the back of my mind that occasionally whispers, "What if I never find the love of my life?"

I'm not talking about a pity party, that well-known gathering of whining, selfishness, and tunnel vision. I'm talking about the gut-level pain of a broken world in which we were created for relationship yet not all matched up in loving pairs. God made us with a deep desire to know and be known, to love and be loved. And when those God-given desires go unmet, it hurts. We hurt.

For years, pride prevented me from confessing to the pain of singleness. It felt like admitting defeat—or at least extreme patheticness. I didn't want to get mired in self-pity or be the recipient of others' pity. While most days I'm very content with my life, there are days when loneliness looms large and when, well, singleness stinks. But the antidote I've found most effective is honesty.

When I'm honest with myself and refuse the urge to paste a happy face on a day or moment or situation that's anything but happy, I'm able to move forward. I remember sitting on the floor several years back and crying over an ex-boyfriend. We'd broken up nearly six months prior, but when I stumbled upon a gift he'd given me when we were dating, a fresh wave of grief overcame me. I allowed myself to stop and grieve the loss of the relationship—and the overall dream of being married by that point in life. In the midst of my tears, I discovered the best part about allowing myself to express these negative emotions: They get out so I can get on with life. It's nice to know there's a healthy middle ground between bottling up these feelings and getting stuck in the oh-woe-is-me stage.

I've also learned the value of being honest with others. A couple years ago, I shared with my singles Bible study a recent struggle with my singleness and how God worked in that situation. After the study was over, three different women in the group told me how much they appreciated my honesty about my struggles with singleness. They could relate. We had some wonderful conversations and left that night feeling encouraged, understood, and not so alone.

Most important, I've started being honest with God. It amazes me that my simple, ineloquent prayers—"God, singleness stinks today. I feel so lonely. Please help."—are answered with such depth of understanding, compassion, and love. No, God doesn't offer human arms to hold us or eyes to gaze lovingly into ours. But when we go to him in vulnerability and honesty and allow him to minister to our very core, he's more than enough.

Take a Cue from the Boy Scouts

While some singleness stinks days are a surprise, others we can see coming from a mile away. There's Valentine's Day, wedding season, the holidays, our birthday. Instead of just bracing ourselves for contact when these days are approaching, my friends and I have discovered a few effective battle plans.

If You Can't Beat 'Em, Join 'Em

Last year on Valentine's Day, The Girls gathered at my roommate's and my apartment for our own little soiree. We had coffee and dessert (a yummy heart-shaped chocolate cake compliments of Kate), and my roommate bought each of us a flower to take home. Instead of sitting home feeling left out or going out and being surrounded by happy couples, we gathered and celebrated on our own turf and terms.

Vacate

As I mentioned in an earlier chapter, last year on Mother's Day some single girlfriends and I went on vacation. And a few years before that a similar group and I traveled over Thanksgiving weekend. Instead of sitting in church and feeling left out while the pastor praised moms on Mother's Day, or sitting at home with paired-off relatives eating turkey and fending off questions about our love life on Thanksgiving, we hopped a plane and avoided the scene altogether. We weren't running from our problems, just mixing it up with a purposeful and positive change of scenery.

Pamper Yourself

A couple years back when five, count 'em, *five* of my cowork-ers were getting married in a one-year period, I was up to here with wedding talk. I was happy for these friends, truly I was. But some days, after listening to discussions about florists, photog-raphers, honeymoons, and dress styles for the umpteenth time, I wanted to run screaming from the building. So on those days, I snuck away to my lunchtime luxury, a local coffee shop, with a great single-girl novel in tow. With a Frappuccino in hand and the single-girl protagonist du jour as my companion, I sipped and read my way through a blissful lunch hour. And upon returning to the office, I was more relaxed and more patient with the next round of wedding talk. Similarly, last summer, when both my friend Lisa and I turned thirty, our friends pitched in and got us gift certificates for a chichi day spa in downtown Chicago. Lisa enjoyed an hour-long massage while I reveled in my manicure and pedicure, and we both discovered it's diffi-cult to bemoan getting older when you're being treated so well.

Facing the Future

While we're being proactive, there are some key questions to ask ourselves: What do I want my life to look like if I'm not mar-ried ten years from now? Or what do I want my life to look like if I never get married? These questions may seem scary, but what's more scary is not asking these questions and just letting life take its course. That's how we get lulled into half-living, like we're in some sort of waiting room. And we all know how bor-ing waiting rooms can be! We're going to set our life course—either actively or passively—as time goes by. How much better to be active with our plans and with our singleness.

So how about it? If you never get to invest time in a husband and kids, what would you want to accomplish, create, build, do, become? Would you want to pursue an advanced degree?

Start your own business? Launch a new ministry? Buy your own home? Live in another country? These dreams may seem big, but the rest of our life is a long time. And when we know where we're headed, we can tackle these dreams in doable increments along the way. Perhaps you could consult your Have, Be, and Do lists and string together a rough five- or ten-year plan.

One great mind-stretching, faith-building exercise is looking at the lives of older single women around us. When we see what they've accomplished in their solo years, we gain insights into the countless possibilities of singleness. Here are a few role models of successful older singles in my life:

Jan

When I started my first job out of college, I found myself in an office next to Jan. I got to know this single woman, who looked far younger than her thirtysomething years, over brainstorming meetings and casual conversations during which she recommended a dentist, doctor, mechanic, and the like to recently transplanted me. She, another single coworker, and I would occasionally go to movies and dinner together, and I would marvel at Jan's employment history. Before joining the editorial staff of *Today's Christian Woman* magazine, she did some architectural design work for both Disney World in Florida and a hotel in Japan. Since leaving *TCW* several years ago, she's served on the staff at a hermitage, been a freelance writer, and edited two different gardening magazines. She's now forty-seven, has a rich work/ministry history behind her ... and who knows what kind of adventures ahead.

Tess and Alison

Alison is a former principal at the school where my mom teaches, and she is now the assistant superintendent for the entire school district. Her housemate, Tess, was in a carpool with my mom when she was getting her masters at the school where Tess is the dean of the school of education. Tess and Alison, both fortysomethings with multiple degrees to their name, share a lovely home in my parents' suburb. They also travel extensively for work (presenting at education seminars in the U.S. and beyond) and for fun, and are both heavily involved in the music program at their church. These classy women have not only pursued their own educational goals over the years, they've passed this passion on to countless other students and teachers.

Susan

I met this out-of-state work contact at a conference years ago, and our shared singleness became an instant bonding point. Now our business phone calls are sprinkled with chats about men, good single-girl books, and milestone birthdays. Susan, who's now forty, started her own publicity company and recently moved from her first house to her second. Just about a month ago, Susan called to check on a story she'd pitched me, but before she got down to business, she simply had to tell me about the guy she'd just started seeing. He's a widower at her church who'd just moved into town. While it was still early in the relationship, there was a hint of giddiness in Susan's voice. "It doesn't matter if you're sixteen, thirty-two, or forty, you still get butterflies," she said of this budding romance. Good to know! It was wonderful to hear this woman, who's wrestled with her singleness as much as any of us, say, "If he's the one, he was definitely worth waiting for." If this is Susan's lifelong love, she definitely won't be the first woman who's found a husband a bit later in life. Every now and then I've heard or read of a woman who found love after thirty or forty or even fifty.

Long-Awaited Love

Several years ago my church held a big anniversary celebration during which many people from the congregation got up and shared stories of how God had worked in their lives during the decades our church has been in existence. Hands down, my favorite story was shared by Dudley and Inge, the couple whose love story is as unusual as their names.

They met more than twenty years ago when they both worked at the same radio station. Inge was friends with Dudley and his wife and kids and even kept in contact with them when she left the country to do missions work overseas. But after hopping around to different assignments, she eventually lost contact with them—for about seventeen years. During that time, Dudley's wife battled ovarian cancer and eventually lost the fight. After her death, Dudley started looking up old friends, including Inge. He finally found her through an Internet search and discovered she was now working in the States. So he called her.

Inge, now forty-six years old, was surprised to hear from Dudley, and when she returned his call, they ended up talking for an hour. It was then she learned of his wife's death and got caught up on the kids, who were in their late teens. Inge had continued her missions work over the years and had never married. "There were a lot of years when it was just God and me," she says, then admits, "It wasn't always easy, but I tried not to wallow in loneliness."

That initial phone conversation triggered a budding e-mail and telephone relationship. Then they finally had a face-to-face reunion, and after they got used to the older versions of

Single Stuff

Without Reservations
by Alice Steinbach

Based on the real-life adventures of the author, who decided not to let being a divorced empty-nester lull her into a mopey or mediocre life. Instead she took a year off from her job (nice for her, a vicarious thrill for us) and lived briefly in Paris and in various parts of Italy and England. She makes interesting observations about womanhood, aging, and singleness as she meets strangers, takes classes, mails herself postcards, breathes in sights famous and obscure, and reinvents herself many miles away from home.

each other, they became a couple. Within months they were engaged, and not long after that they got married.

Dudley says, "I'd always admired Inge's relationship with God, even back when we first worked together. It was always, 'Jesus and me. We'll get through this together.'"

"Now it's Jesus and Dudley and me," Inge says with a smile, then adds, "It's worth waiting for the right person. In all my forty-six years of singleness, I knew it was better to be single and wishing to be married than married and wishing to be single. But in our years of marriage, I haven't once wanted to be single again." That's a sentiment Dudley wholeheartedly seconds.

Holding Out Hope

What's great about both Susan's and Inge's stories is that they're much-needed reminders of a wonderful truth: We never know what's going to happen tomorrow. Both were taken off guard by romance well after they'd thought they'd never find it. But both fortysomethings agree it's well worth the wait to find healthy, God-honoring, lasting love—no matter how long that wait may be.

This presents probably one of the most tricky dichotomies of the single life. We don't want to place so much hope in marriage that we put all our eggs in that future basket and fail to live life fully now. And yet we don't want to be so hopeless, thinking the chance for love has passed us by, that we get jaded and bitter. Somewhere between these two extremes is a healthy, precarious balance. But it's difficult to hold on to this delicate brand of hope, especially as the years go by.

So how do you make the most of singleness when deep down the desire of your heart is to be married? I think the secret lies in an often-misunderstood verse in Psalms: "Delight yourself in the LORD and he will give you the desires of your heart" (37:4). So often we get fixated on the latter part of this verse—the desires of our heart—that we gloss over the key: delighting in the Lord. When delighting in the One who made us, loves us unconditionally, knows the number of hairs on our head, counts our every tear, seeks us out, and saves us becomes the primary focus of our life, we're able to look to the future with hope. When we place our heart in his hands, he's free to shape our desires to match his will and lead us down whatever unique, adventure-laden path he has for each of us. It's only then that we realize our joy and heart's desire really are contingent on one man—not Mr. Right, but Jesus.

What's So Great about Being Single?

If you're still having trouble seeing the up side of singleness, get a load of the following list compiled from informal questioning of marrieds and singles alike. It's even in a handy clip-and-save format for those inevitable singleness stinks days.

 We can make spur-of-the-moment plans.

 And when we do, we don't have to call home and check with anyone to make sure it's okay.

 We can squeeze our toothpaste tube any ol' way we want to.

 We can read in bed as late as we want to without the light bothering anyone.

 We're still allowed to flirt.

 We still get to experience the rush of new love.

 We can read the Bible early in the morning or late at night and not bother anyone else.

We can hog the covers, the closet space, the ice cream, and the remote.

 We can deal with our "issues" without having to subject someone else to the process.

 In winter, we can go weeks without shaving our legs and no one knows.

 We're free to invest all kinds of time and energy in missions trips, the church nursery, the youth group, Habitat for Humanity, literacy programs, etc.

 We're still allowed to notice cute boys.

 We can borrow clothes from our roommates.

 We can talk aloud to God while we do the dishes . . . and no one looks at us funny.

 If we buy floral sheets, no one complains.

When we bring a "chick flick" home from Blockbuster, no one rolls their eyes.

 We can wear sweats to bed and no one's disappointed.

 Instead of investing a lion's share of our love and attention on one person, we can lavish it on numerous friends and family members.

 We can play with, cuddle, and spoil other people's children, then give them back when they get whiny or poopy.

 There are no in-laws to attempt to get along with.

 We can go where we want on vacation.

 We're not forced to endure televised football, basketball, baseball, golf, bowling . . .

 All the hairs in the tub drain are ours.

Our toilet seat is always down.

According to Hollywood, we single chicks are trendy.

 We don't have to justify the purchase of another pair of black shoes to anyone (except maybe God!).

 There's no moose head hanging on our wall or overstuffed plaid Lazy Boy from the eighties parked in our living room.

 The joy of Me Nights.

 The joy of Girls' Night Out without the guilt of leaving a hubby or kids at home.

 There are a few less balls to juggle (a husband and kids) in this fast-paced, multipressured world.

 We still have the first kiss with our future husband to look forward to.

 We're free to explore all the talents and dreams God's wired in us.

 No matter what the future holds, we can have the security of knowing we can stand on our own two feet.

 Like the apostle Paul, we're free to have "undivided devotion to the Lord" (1 Cor. 7:33).

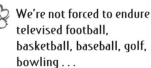

Now it's your turn to come up with some perks to the single life. Add to this list, or better yet, compose your own. If you have trouble, grab a single girlfriend and brainstorm together (some sort of gooey chocolate treat would probably help too!).